THE EVIL EMPIRE

GLOBALIZATION'S DARKER SIDE

PAUL HELLYER

Chimo Media

Canadian Cataloguing in Publication Data

Hellyer, Paul, 1923-
 The evil empire: globalization's darker side

Includes bibliographical references and index.
ISBN 0-9694394-5-8

1. Canada — Economic policy — 1991-   I. Title.

HC115.H44 1997   330.971   C97-932294-4

Printed and bound in Canada. The paper used in this book is acid free.

Chimo Media Limited
99 Atlantic Ave., Suite 302
Toronto, ON M6K 3J8
Canada (416) 535-7611

CONTENTS

ACKNOWLEDGMENTS

As always, I am deeply grateful to a number of individuals and organizations for their assistance in the preparation of this book. I am indebted to, Don Champagne, Harold Chorney, Jim Jordan, Wm. Hixson, Wm. Krehm, Mike McCracken and Ian Woods for reading the draft manuscript. Their comments and suggestions have been invaluable both in respect of content and presentation. In addition they helped me to avoid myriad errors and omissions. Responsibility for those that slipped through, and for the views expressed, rests with me alone.

I am especially grateful to Terry Prout for his understanding yet decisive editing. His ability to sort the wheat from the chaff was most helpful.

Once again my executive assistant, Nina Moskaliuk, deserves a special word of praise for all her help. She was painstaking in her research and indefatigable in recording and revising the text, chapter by chapter.

Andy Donato wins another prize for his insightful cartoon. He has captured the essence of the threat that globalization poses to Canadian sovereignty.

Thanks to Rachel Mansfield for preparing the index with her usual meticulous care.

A number of organizations were especially cooperative and gracious in lending assistance. These include the Parliamentary Library in Ottawa, the Metropolitan Reference Library, the United States Consulate in Toronto and the Public Affairs Department of the Bank of England. To each and all, my grateful thanks.

Finally I would like to thank my family one more time. They, and especially my wife Ellen, have paid a high price for my continued interest in political and economic affairs.

FOREWORD

Do you ever get the sense that something you fear and dislike is happening but you can't quite put your finger on what it is? Values are changing. Life is becoming more of a rat race. People seem to count less and money has become the focus of our lives and political structures. Money is driving our governments and now it wants to rule the world.

The reason it is so difficult to put a handle on what is happening is that the manipulators of money have jammed our consciousness to the point of hypnosis by playing their broken record over, and over and over again — the deficit is the problem; we have to cut back; we have been living beyond our means; the unemployed could find work if they really wanted to; governments don't create jobs; short-term pain is essential for long-term gain; once we get the fundamentals right all will be well; bigger is better; globalization is inevitable and will be good for Canada and the world.

This broken record, imported duty-free but certainly not pain-free, from the Chicago School of Economics, has been playing incessantly for so long that most Canadians have come to accept its superficial analysis and twisted logic as truth. So much so that we have become a nation of masochists taking satisfaction from our self-inflicted punishment.

This short book examines the cracks in the broken record. Heresy to some, I hope it will be judged more favorably by those who reflect carefully on its message. Contrary to what we have been told, the deficit was not "the problem" but rather a symptom of much deeper problems; the only reason we have lived beyond our means is because our economic managers forced us to produce far less than we were capable of doing. There was no real need to close hospitals and cutback essential services; the product of short-term pain has been long-term pain — not gain; the vast majority of the unemployed would like to work if they could find a job; governments have and can create jobs; bigger is not necessarily better as it leads to "monopoly" with fewer jobs and higher prices; and globalization as presently conceived is neither good for Canada nor the rest of the world. It is the embryo of the "Evil Empire".

Globalization is simply a code word to camouflage what is really going on. Globalization is not about trade, as its promoters would like us to believe, it is about power and control. It is an attempt by the largest international banks and multinational corporations to run the world their way, for their own benefit and by their own set of rules, rules that would allow them to undo a century of social progress and to alter the distribution of income from inequitable to inhuman. In fact the empire they plan would be an evil empire in the truest sense. It would be an empire where individual countries, especially the small ones, would lose the flexibility to pass good and humane laws in the interests of all the people. Gold would be the absolute monarch and goodness a mark of disloyalty.

This evil empire is not a figment of the imagination. Plans are well advanced and it will become a reality unless we take immediate steps to stop it.

CHAPTER 1

LOST IN THE FOREST

"Democracy is on trial in the world, on a more colossal scale than ever before."

Charles Fletcher Dole

While flying from Toronto to Regina about a week before the general election of June 2, 1997, Saskatoon lawyer Doug Richardson spotted me and slipped across the aisle into the empty seat beside me. Doug is an old Ottawa buff who had been prime minister John Turner's chief of staff, so the subject of mutual interest was politics. In the course of a business trip to Toronto he had been taking the city's political pulse and was interested in my reading of the situation.

After we reviewed the several party leaders, their platforms and performances, I asked Doug if he had ever been lost in a forest. I had been, deep in the woods of my beloved Muskoka district, and it was a terrifying experience not to know which way I was going or which way I should be going to reach my destination safely. Lost in the forest, I said, was where our political leaders are today — worse, they are relying on a broken compass to point the way out.

The broken compass comprises the views of bankers and bureaucrats who have been deeply influenced by Nobel laureate Milton Friedman and his former colleagues in the economics department at the University of Chicago. They have adopted the "Chicago School" as holy writ and defend it with a passion even in the face of its miserable track record — people like the governor of the Bank of Canada and the deputy minister of finance who lead the government around by the nose and who have reduced the role of successive prime ministers and finance ministers to that of mere puppets. Doug Richardson remembered the tremendous power exercised by the bureaucratic establishment because he had seen it with his own eyes when he was executive assistant to Liberal Finance Minister Marc Lalonde in 1982. He also knew that taking the bureaucracy on for size would be as difficult as attacking a nest of enemy machine gunners; but it is the only way to recapture common sense.

The conversation then turned to what might be possible if we approached our social and economic problems with open minds. What if we rated people as important as money, for example? That would be a switch from the present course. And what about a fairer deal for the people who create real wealth in the form of goods and services rather than loading the dice in favor of those who simply make money by playing with money? The current trend shrieks with injustice. As he left to return to his seat Doug said: "You make a convincing case."

It is a convincing case for anyone who will take the time to listen and whose mind is open to all possibilities. But even the skeptics should be sure they know which way the needle is pointing. Mere movement is not necessarily progress. It is imperative to know where we are coming from and where we are headed. Should we just plough ahead or should we do an about turn and retrace our steps to the point of entry? The answer lies in what kind of country and what kind of world we want. So, perhaps, it may be useful to simulate a helicopter view of the kind of world we are exiting and the very different kind of world that awaits us if we continue on through the forest without a radical change in direction.

THE WORLD WE ARE LEAVING BEHIND

The world we are leaving behind is the progressive world of the post-World War II era. Following on the heels of one of the greatest economic depressions of all time, it was a matter of public policy to do everything possible to make sure that jobs were available for anyone who really wanted to work. Optimism filled the air.

The veterans' charter made it possible for those who had served in the armed forces to attend university at public expense and the same philosophy helped keep tuition fees low in subsequent years so that post-secondary education was open to all economic groups.

Compassion was a Canadian trademark and financial assistance was made available to the disadvantaged and helpless. A health care system was established which provided universal access to treatment for everyone and tighter environmental standards were developed to protect the health of present and future generations. We were also generous in assisting people of other countries.

There were "four pillars" in the financial world — banks, trust, brokerage and insurance companies and there was some limited competition among them. The distribution of income contributed to a growing middle-class as the Canadian dream of equal opportunity for all moved toward reality.

THE WORLD TO COME

As a result of Chicago School and laissez-faire economics we have already moved to the point where full employment is no longer deemed either possible or desirable. The Bank of Canada simply will not allow the kind of rapid economic growth required to reduce the rate much below 8.0 per cent. Indeed in the Fall of 1997 it began to raise interest rates to slow the economy while we were still stuck at the 9% level.

Post-secondary education is becoming increasingly inaccessible to anyone except the well-to-do. Students accumulate debts of $10,000 to $25,000 before graduation and often with no job to go to. We are fast developing a two-tier health care system where the best care is only available to the rich. We are eliminating competition between financial institutions by allowing the banks to buy everything in sight, and we try to control inflation by means of interest rates alone. This is resulting in a monumental transfer of income from poor to rich. It is also creating a mountain of debt — governmental, corporate and personal. And that debt will rise until the system collapses, once again.

AN EVIL WIND

As alarming as the above list of changes may be to those of us who look back with nostalgia on a fairer more compassionate era, they are only the tip of the iceberg — a harbinger of things to come. As the late September wind hints of the inevitability of winter, there are more changes in the air which warn of tremendous hardship and heartache in the years ahead.

The Canadian government has been aggressively promoting a treaty called the Multilateral Agreement on Investment (MAI) which has been negotiated in great secrecy by the 29-nation Organization for Economic Cooperation and Development (OECD) at its headquarters in Paris, France. Originally slated for signature in the Spring of 1997, the current deadline for approval is sometime in the Spring of 1998.

To understand the worrisome import of the treaty it is helpful to know who its sponsors are. It began with the United States Council for International Business which recruited the U.S. government as its stalking horse. Along the way it has gained the support of international banks and multinational corporations, including some in Canada, which appear to have a hundred times more influence with governments than ordinary citizens can muster.

The MAI, which is being well camouflaged in the innocuous cloak of globalism, is in reality a bill of rights for international banks and the multinational corporations they control. An attempt was made to introduce it through the World Trade Organization but it failed when many of the small Third-World countries objected. They did not want to transfer their sovereign rights concerning who might invest in their countries and who might not to an unelected world organization run by big business. Undaunted the MAI's promoters decided to switch their effort to the Organization for Economic Cooperation and Development comprising 29 of the world's richest countries. Once they have signed the treaty the poorer countries will have their arms twisted one by one under threat of being denied access to foreign capital.

So far the strategy has worked well. Two years of secret negotiation has resulted in agreement in principal with only the details remaining to be worked out. There has been little opposition because both citizens and their elected representatives have been kept in the dark. The whole operation has been limited to governments and bureaucrats.

If the MAI is signed it will give to foreign individuals and businesses all of the investment rights enjoyed by Canadian citizens. It would eliminate our right to attach conditions as we did when pharmaceutical companies were required to do research in Canada in exchange for a break on patent protection. There would be no limit on the extent of foreign investment and soon access would be given to previously restricted areas such as telecommunications, financial institutions and culture.

The treaty would make it impossible for Canadian legislators, either federal or provincial, to alter or improve environmental standards for fear of being sued by multinational corporations whether operating in Canada or not. Equally repugnant, the treaty would encourage multinationals to reverse a century of social progress by moving production to countries that allow sweatshops and child labor in the knowledge that there would be nothing we could do to prevent those products from entering Canada.

What we are talking about is a virtual world without borders ruled by a virtual dictatorship of the world's most powerful central banks, commercial banks and multinational companies. It would be a world where small countries like Canada don't count, a world where our legislators would count for even less, and where citizens as voters would count for nothing at all because it wouldn't matter who we elected. Government, any government, would be almost powerless to affect and improve our destiny.

The world described above is an absolute certainty if we just sit on our hands and do nothing. So anyone content with a vision of that kind of world can just relax and "enjoy it" as the inevitable unfolds. For those who find the prospect frightening and totally unacceptable, immediate, concerted action is required. Soon, very soon, it will be too late.

CHAPTER 2

THE AMERICAN MODEL

"The main enemy of the open society, I believe, is no longer the communist but the capitalist threat. "

George Soros

T hose of us who are old enough to remember the early post-World War II years remember them fondly. In both Canada and the United States prospects looked and felt good. Veterans had little difficulty finding a niche in the civilian world. Tens of thousands of farmers moved to the cities and found jobs while hundreds of thousands of immigrants, from the four corners of the earth, were equally blessed. Of course the struggle wasn't always easy but there was always a path of opportunity available if you searched for it.

This post-war prosperity was widely shared. Labor earned significant wage gains and they were mainly real because inflation was modest. Capital was adequately rewarded for its contribution to increased output and governments flourished. On both sides of the 49th parallel the proportion of federal debt to Gross Domestic Product (GDP) fell dramatically from a wartime high.

Little wonder that the fifteen years following the Korean War are remembered as the "golden years". The ideas of John Maynard Keynes reigned supreme and for the first time in almost 200 years economic theory and the operation of the real economy appeared to be in harmony.

In 1961, long before the honeymoon had ended, a small black cloud appeared on the economic horizon. It was the increasing concentration of power in big business and big labor and the increasing propensity to use their market power (monopoly power) in a way that was sure to rock the economic boat. It didn't take long for the small black cloud to develop into a major storm warning. By the mid-1960s the wage-price spiral had begun in earnest. Wages increased by a multiple of average productivity growth, so costs rose. Prices were quick to follow. Then the higher prices became the rationale for even further wage demands. It became a never-ending circle.

Orthodox economists attributed this new phenomenon, with its inflationary consequences, to the Vietnam War. U.S. President Lyndon Johnson had launched his great society program while the Vietnam War was still being waged. At the same time he had not raised taxes to siphon-off the increase in purchasing power.

What economists did not explain then, and have not explained to this day, is why the wage-price spiral actually began in Canada and the United Kingdom at least a year before it did in the U.S. It began in different countries at different times for different reasons and would appear to have little if any connection to the Vietnam War. Failure to recognize and admit this fact may account for a major blind spot in the subsequent revolution in economic theory.

In any event the wage-price spiral put central banks in an invidious position. If they increased the money supply fast enough to clear the market of goods and services, at ever higher prices, there would be soaring inflation. If they restricted the money growth to a normal increase there would be massive unemployment. In practice most of them compromised and produced too much unemployment and too much inflation at the same time. The late Swedish Nobel laureate Gunnar Myrdal coined the world "stagflation" to describe this unprecedented state of economic affairs. In the course of an interview he told me that he didn't understand the reasons for stagflation, which surprised me, because there didn't seem to be any great secret involved.

In the late '60s and early '70s there were numerous attempts to control the wage-price spiral by means of an incomes policy. A number of these worked quite successfully for a while — several for a number of years — but in the end they all failed. They failed, in my opinion, for predictable reasons. Many were voluntary and consequently doomed from the outset. Others had bureaucrats setting individual wages and prices. This system has never worked except briefly during an emergency such as wartime. Nor will it ever work in a market economy because the data on which prices are based change constantly. Still other experiments distributed the benefits of technology on the basis of specific industries which was both unfair and seen to be unfair because some groups profited while others did not. Inevitably the practice led to failure and abandonment.

Instead of examining the reasons for failure and attempting new experiments based on that experience, which would have been a logical course, mainline economics threw out the baby with the bath water. It turned its back on Keynesian economics and demand management which had served us so well in the early post-war years. It rejected incomes policies, even though they were still in their infancy, and turned to money as a single powerful regulator of economic activity.

MONETARISM

It is ironic that the new wave economics, which has been called the monetarist counter-revolution, should emanate from the economics department of the University of Chicago. Professor Milton Friedman and his colleagues developed the theories known as monetarism which became the predominant "economic religion" of the late 20th century.

The irony is that Friedman and his associates were steeped in the tradition of the Chicago School of the 1930s, which produced some of the best economic thinking ever, but by some inexplicable process managed to abandon that tradition of excellence to produce some of the worst, most destructive ideas ever to hit the world stage. That the majority of mainline economists have accepted these ideas as "holy writ" is one of the greatest tragedies of all time.

The mathematics of monetarism is based on two fundamental assumptions. First, that we have a pure market economy in which all prices obey the law of supply and demand and, second, that all inflation is monetary inflation and that there is no other kind. Consequently all you have to do is get the right size nozzle on the money supply and some kind of equilibrium — some invisible hand, no doubt — will regulate all facets of the economy in the most efficient and acceptable manner. Neither of these fundamental tenets is correct but because they have been accepted as legitimate for so long, a very heavy economic and social toll has been exacted.

Monetarism gained tacit acceptance in 1974 and that year marked the great divide in economic performance. The rate of growth of the U.S. economy fell dramatically from an average annual increase in Gross National Product of 3.70% from 1948 to 1973, to 2.28% annual increase in Gross Domestic Product from 1974 to 1993. The increase in per capita disposable income fell from 2.45% to 1.32% for the same period, while average annual hourly earnings dropped from an increase of 2.19% to a decrease of 0.73 per cent.[1]

These figures, as stark as they are, mask a far bigger change in late 20th-century America. A massive redistribution of wealth has occurred. The top 1% of households now own 47% of shareholder equity while the bottom 80% of households own only 2 per cent. This represents an enormously increased inequality. Shareholders have been reaping huge benefits while people who do the productive work essential to create real wealth struggle to stay afloat. It is a system which threatens to self-destruct by undermining long-term social stability both in America and in other parts of the world.

UNREGULATED LAISSEZ-FAIRE CAPITALISM

At the G-7 summit in Denver, Colorado, in June 1997, President Clinton touted the American economy as a model for the world. True, it has enjoyed seven years of steady growth and the number of jobs created has been formidable. The other side of the coin is less rosy. The economy is quite capable of operating in the 3.5% annual growth range, rather than 2.5%, but the Federal Reserve Board will not allow it. And the unemployment rate could have been much lower than the current 4.8% — which in itself is a misleadingly low figure.

Of even greater long-term significance is the renewed tough stance toward labor. "Our firms can fire; so they hire," says C. Fred Bergsten, director of the Institute for International Economics in Washington. "Japanese and German firms can't fire; so they don't hire." Bergsten argues that the U.S. model "is definitely better for everybody. In a world where all companies have to compete globally, you have to get with it in terms of market-oriented approaches, or you will suffer."[2] Nevertheless there are many sociologists who believe that extreme labor flexibility is just another way of describing the 19th-century style capitalism where workers were hired when needed and dumped like so many over-ripe cabbages when they weren't — the kind of capitalism that led to trade unionism in some countries and communism or fascism in others.

The current success of American firms in downsizing, restructuring and merging is having a devastating effect on American workers. When Robert E. Allen, AT&T's chairman ordered 40,000 jobs cut from the payroll, at a time when the company appeared to be doing very well financially, his action struck a hornets nest of opposition. Stung by the criticism of his compensation package, Allen responded with a testy letter to all employees.[3] (One wonders what kind of reaction he expected.) His ruthlessness was consistent with the message from financial markets which is, "go for maximum short-term gain or get out."

"Al Dunlop was the CEO of Scott Paper Co., for two years. During that time he eliminated the jobs of 11,000 people and put them out on the street with no prospects of any future. He cut research and development in half, sharply cutback expenditures on staff training and cut out all contributions to any kind of community charity. He also told the managers in the company that they were not to participate in any sort of voluntary community service because if they had any extra time and energy available it should go into the company. The value of Scott Paper shares went up roughly 220%; added something on the order of $6 billion to the shareholder value of the company. For two years work he walked off with $100 million in compensation."[4] The American dream for some ... an American nightmare for thousands.

There are, of course, many executives who act responsibly toward their employees and are good citizens in their communities. Should their companies be viewed as under-performers, however, they are often asked to move on and make way for one of the hatchetmen. That is the reality of a market that is obsessed with short-term results and an open invitation for executives to act ruthlessly. Workers who lose their jobs, and even those who don't but who have had their wages frozen or in some cases actually rolled back, are not unaware of the double standard under which the compensation of CEOs may rise dramatically.

Another important change with uncertain long-term effects is the loss of worker loyalty. I have talked to several people whose companies have merged with others — in some cases with former, fierce competitors. They now go to work and do what is required of them because a paycheck is involved. But they no longer go the second mile and would walk out in a minute if a better offer came along. Nor do they push the team spirit. The "me first, and to hell with my neighbor" attitude seems to be spilling down from the CEOs to the lower ranks.

Without in any way dismissing the importance of jobs and GDP, it is correct to say that there is more to life. There is habitat, for example. Humans are one of the few species known for fouling their own nest. Soon after President Clinton had bragged to the G-7 that the American model was the one to emulate, he admitted to the United Nations Earth Summit that "high growth" policies had foiled hopes of reducing the greenhouse gas emissions which are altering the world climate. "No nation can escape this danger — we must all do our part," he said, while noting that the U.S., with just 4% of the world's population, produces 20% of the world's greenhouse gases.[5] It would have been more precise to say that unregulated capitalism pays minimum heed to the common good whether it be clean air, clean water, clean beaches or just about anything else that doesn't show up on the profit side of the bottom line.

FOREIGN POLICY

If the extension of membership in the North Atlantic Treaty Organization had nothing to do with world security and everything to do with U.S. domestic politics, as Prime Minister Jean Chrétien blurted out in his supposedly private but overheard conversation with Belgian Prime Minister Jean-Luc Dehaene, it leads to two very important questions.[6] Why did Canada go along with it when the cost will be a few hundred million dollars? And does U.S. domestic politics rule the world?

The Eastern Caribbean's banana industry is in crisis because the U.S. used political muscle to benefit powerful corporate citizens who operate massive banana plantations in Latin America. In response to a U.S.-driven complaint, the World Trade Organization in April, 1997, ordered the 15-nation European Union to change its banana import system which guaranteed former and current French colonies a share of the European market and imposed quotas on Latin American growers.[7] It is a clear case of primarily small, independent farmers fearing they will be driven into the ground by larger U.S.-owned growers such as Dole, Del Monte and Chiquita. It is a foretaste of what U.S. foreign policy is doing and plans to do to the world through trading and investment treaties including the World Trade Organization, the FTA, NAFTA and now the MAI.

Opening up the world to unrestricted trade sounds like

a wonderful idea. Competition will increase and prices come down. But that is the short-term view. You can be sure that if the small Caribbean banana growers are squeezed out of business they will have little choice other than to sell their land to the giants and then accept employment at substandard wages. What we are talking about is not world trade as an end in itself, but rather world trade as a means of achieving world hegemony. Free trade needs to be "fair" trade, or else it will end up being tyrannical.

In their relentless pursuit of bigger is better the Americans (and Americanized-Canadians) have forgotten one of the most important lessons in history. The unregulated capitalism of the late-nineteenth century may have produced a lot of wealth but it didn't create utopia, far from it. John D. Rockefeller, for example, wasn't guided by the altruism of an invisible hand when he bought most of the small oil companies. He did it because he didn't like competition and his fine hand can still be seen by those Canadians naive enough to wonder why gasoline prices increase across the board on a Thursday afternoon before a long weekend. When gasoline prices rose dramatically in August, 1997, I asked for an explanation from someone familiar with the business. "Greed," was the reply. "Greed made possible by oligopoly."

Eventually, however, the Americans realized there was a problem with too much concentration of power. Anti-trust laws were enacted and used to break up companies like AT&T and Standard Oil. But now, after years of deregulation, anti-trust is in hibernation and official "thinking" has reverted to that of the late-nineteenth century. Gone, and almost forgotten, are the fifteen years following the Korean War when the U.S. economy was most productive, when labor was reasonably paid, when the distribution of income was not absurdly unequal and when everyone was reasonably happy and upbeat. That level of comfort cannot be duplicated in the absence of appropriate regulation.

The other equally profound lesson that U.S. officials and economists have forgotten is that a fractional reserve banking system will ultimately lead to an economic meltdown as it has so many times in the past. Certainly there are a plethora of books predicting another crash but there is precious little discussion in the media or by politicians as to why that is likely to happen. The reason is simple. If all or nearly all of the new money created each year is created in the form of debt by privately owned banks, and interest must be paid on all that debt, and no one creates any money with which to pay the interest, further borrowing is required just to pay the interest on what is already owed. Total debt increases, and when the debt increases faster than the economy grows, as it currently does, a meltdown is inevitable.

Keith Helmuth has a novel way of explaining the debt problem caused by compound interest. "At this point there are two obvious questions: (1) Isn't the money that exists needed for circulation in the productive economy until such time as it goes to pay back the loans which created it, and (2) if a part of the money which is in circulation in the productive economy is used to satisfy compound interest charges, (for which no corresponding money has been created) won't there be a short-fall in the ability of the productive economy to repay the debt it had previously contracted? The answer to both questions is, "yes". Under this arrangement the financial system captures back more money than it created. Capital accumulates in the financial sector and is depleted in the productive sector. The working capital of the productive economy is like a flock of chickens in the farmyard of society. Compound interest is like a chicken hawk which periodically swoops in, nabs a hen, and takes it out of production."[8] Eventually we will run out of hens.

Not only is the U.S. the world's biggest debtor, its federal debt is now about $5-trillion, but Congress will soon have to face the music once again and raise the statutory limit. Worse, the U.S. total non-financial debt — federal, state, municipal, corporate and personal — is roughly $15-trillion or about 190% of Gross Domestic Product. The interest rate on that debt must be about twice as high, on average, as the growth rate of the economy. So, you don't need a Ph.D. in economics to know that if you owe almost twice as much as you earn, and the rate of interest on what you owe is twice as high as your annual increase in income, you have a problem, a serious problem!

The inevitable meltdown may be postponed for a while by the amount of debt that is being wiped off the books each year. U.S. personal bankruptcies soared 27% in 1996 to a record number and people obtain swift discharges from revolving-courtroom doors, and then go speedily into debt again. In earlier times people resisted bankruptcy because of shame but now, consistent with laissez-faire, it is almost fashionable to go bust and start all over again.

For the future there are two fundamental problems to be faced. First, is the insatiable appetite for growth by multinational companies which want to dominate markets worldwide. And second, the allied problem of a monetary system that is both unstable and unsustainable. Both of these problems will have to be addressed and resolved if we want an economic model to emulate.

CHAPTER 3

A MEDIOCRE CANADA

*"If the people of the nation understood our banking
and monetary system, I believe there would be a
revolution before tomorrow morning. "*

Henry Ford, Sr.

I have always been extremely proud of Canada's
achievements during World War II and in the post-war period.
We were transformed from an agricultural society into a widely
diversified one. The war years got us into manufacturing and
science. The post-war period saw our greatest flowering as our
newly developed affluence allowed us to add both a social safety
net and substantial support for the arts to our broad range of
pursuits.

We had little difficulty financing this wide diversity until
our system was struck with the monetarist virus and many of
our best programs came under attack or were cancelled
altogether. This is not mere coincidence. The monetarist
dogma, including the private bank monopoly on the creation of
new money, leads inevitably to mediocrity.

The erosion was slow at first and difficult to pinpoint.
But the pace quickened and the last few years has seen Canada

abandon its climb to excellence and change direction completely as it turned downhill on the slippery road to second class. We have been slashing, trashing and dismantling programs that took years or decades to develop. It is a Canadian tragedy without precedent because none of the carnage is the result of any natural disaster beyond our control. We have done it to ourselves.

HEALTH CARE

One of the saddest spectacles has been the unravelling of our health care system. Despite the inevitable abuse, it has been Canada's crown jewel. Its bedrock philosophy that all citizens be treated equally has set us apart from our American cousins. We lost our fear of the financial consequences of illness. But now that confidence is being eroded as service is being cutback, queues are lengthening and a two-tier system is gradually evolving.

Dozens of hospitals are being closed right across the country. Some people say that the purpose of the closings is not to save money but to provide a more rational delivery of service. But after talking to dozens of people in the health-care business I have concluded that the only ones who believe the official "explanation" are people who also believe in the tooth fairy. What is happening can best be described as madness — madness born of economic insanity.

Some of the hospitals that will be assigned additional responsibilities when other hospitals close are already unable to cope. On Sunday, February 9, 1997, at Sunnybrook Health Science Centre, decorating consultant Mary Lippert and her husband Chris decided that the time had come for his life support system to be withdrawn. When doctors double-checked that this was indeed their wish, it was done and Chris was moved from the cardiology ward, where he had received superb attention, to the oncology ward. There the level of care changed dramatically for the worse.

Chris Lippert was settled in a semi-private room at 2:30 p.m., where his vital signs were checked. A minute or two later a nurse came in to say: "I'm your nurse, I hope there will be time to get back." No one came until 7:00 p.m. when the nurse returned to renew "the drip". But nothing else was done even though his discomfort was painfully acute. At 8:45 p.m., after doing everything she could to help, Mary could take it no longer. She went to the desk to request a phone number of a private nurse. Every attempt was made to discourage her but she insisted that help was needed "now!". As she attempted to phone she noticed out of the corner of her eye that two nurses had gone to Chris's room. He was given a sponge bath, pulled up in his bed and made comfortable for his last night.[1]

If this were an isolated incident one would hesitate to report it. But it isn't. There have been other similar stories. It may be that a 12-hour shift is just too long and that the nurses get tired. After all, no one can maintain a high energy level for that long. But it is also a certainty that many hospitals are understaffed and consequently many nurses are overworked.

In June, the same hospital admitted blame in the sudden death of a 52-year-old machinist who had survived a horrific accident and then a serious blood shortage. It was alleged that it took almost 10 minutes for someone to answer the floor alarm that went off when Marcello Stirpe went into cardiac arrest. Hospital officials admitted later that Stirpe died as a result of a "breakdown in the monitoring of a patient."[2]

A number of incidents including the fatal fire in Sunnybrook's "K" Wing led the Ontario Nurses to call for a public inquiry into patient care at the hospital. "The events at Sunnybrook raise serious questions about the impact of budget cuts and the current provincial government's policies on health care," said Lesley Bell, RN, Chief Executive Officer of the Ontario Nurses' Association, the union representing 45,000 registered nurses and allied health professionals in Ontario.

"The registered nurses at Sunnybrook have repeatedly brought forward their concerns about workload and under-staffing issues, and have expressed the growing fear that budget cuts are impeding their ability to provide quality care," Bell added.

"If problems related to workload are occurring at one of the top-rated health-care institutions in Canada, imagine what the impact of budget cuts and the government's current policies on health-care is having on the delivery of health services in other hospitals across the province."[3]

That is the point exactly. The Minister of Health and hospital administrators have claimed that the quality of health-care services in Ontario has not been impacted by budget cuts. Nurses say that it has. The nurses are right! Private conversations with numerous patients have confirmed that. Administrators and others who claim otherwise are sleep-walking.

Not only are nurses overworked, and the quality of care eroding, there are other non-sensical developments. I hear reports of idle surgeons and unused operating rooms because quotas for the month have been filled. Queues for elective surgery are growing — including some conditions which are life-threatening. Patients are being released from hospitals too soon and often have to fend for themselves when they are physically and emotionally incapable of doing so. Home-care is being provided by people without adequate training and so on.

Some impatient people who can afford it go to the U.S. for treatment. Others find some means of beating the system. The rich hire their own nurses for home-care. The poor go without. Increasingly a two-tier system is evolving — one for the rich and one for the poor. Inevitably the allegation is made that neo-conservatives want to scrap our system and adopt one closer to the American model. True or not, our system is not the shining jewel it once was.

EDUCATION

This is a subject on which I feel very strongly. I was one of the thousands of veterans who had part or all of their post-secondary education paid at public expense. Universities bulged at the seams and some of the classes were far larger than ideal but the federal government of the day gave us an opportunity that would not have been available otherwise.

The benefit to the country would be difficult to assess but I have never met anyone who doubted that it was one of Canada's best investments. Graduates contributed in a myriad of pursuits and helped Canada achieve its reputation for excellence which is now being fast eroded.

With the benefit of the post-war experience you would think that our policy-makers would bend heaven and earth to make post-secondary education readily accessible to all qualified students no matter what their economic circumstances. Instead, we are moving in the opposite direction toward a more elitist society.

In an article by Brad Lavigne, national chairperson of the Canadian Federation of Students, we are reminded that "student debt in Canada has reached epidemic proportions. About 60 per cent of all full-time students need to borrow in order to attend college and university. The average debt load for these hundreds of thousands of students at graduation has grown from $8,700 in 1990 to $22,000 in 1997. This burden is expected to reach $25,000 within the next two years.

"The reasons for the debt explosion are clear. Since 1993, the federal government has cut $2.29-billion in transfers to the provinces for postsecondary education, tuition fees have increased by 45 per cent and provincial governments have either significantly reduced student grants or eliminated them altogether."[4]

Not only is post-secondary education becoming less accessible to the poor, but the quality of education at the elementary and secondary levels is being affected by budgetary cutbacks as well. In some schools the music program is being eliminated. In others it is the home economics course — currently called family studies. Supplies are also limited. In fact, in some cases things have gotten so bad that teachers have been dipping into their own pockets to buy books and stationery.

Class sizes have been growing and, while this may have been necessary 50 years ago when there was a shortage of teachers, there is no excuse for it today. Teachers report that with classes of 30 or more it is impossible to provide the kind of individual attention required for each student to move forward at his or her potential. Progress for an average student is slower in larger classes and the opportunity for challenged students is markedly reduced. If the future of a country lies in the capacity of its human resources, our penny-pinching approach to education is short-sighted in the extreme.

Library facilities, too, are being reduced. The number of new books being acquired each year is, in many cases, dramatically reduced. Hours of operations have been curtailed. The number of staff available has been cut. All of the above make it more rather than less difficult for students to complete their assignments on time.

The sad conclusion is that our full potential is not being achieved as we turn our backs on the excellence we long pursued; and while the new scholarship program just announced by Prime Minister Chrétien for the year 2000 is welcome, it is only a small step in the right direction.

THE ENVIRONMENT

When the necessity for protecting our world habitat has been so meticulously defined and clearly stated you would think we would be moving full steam ahead. Instead we are procrastinating and back-tracking. Federal and provincial governments have cutback many programs for environmental protection and improvement.

The Great Lakes clean-up is a typical and profoundly disturbing example. Millions of people drink the water from the lakes which also play critical roles in commerce and recreation. Yet the time-table for clean-up and water quality improvements has been set back due to budgetary restrictions. It is a prime example of our warped priorities.

One of Canada's ecological heirlooms is the Niagara Escarpment, a 725-kilometre stretch of limestone and gravel extending from Queenston Heights, on the Niagara River, to Tobermory at the top of the Bruce Peninsula, north of Owen Sound. Safeguards that were put in place by the government of Bill Davis in early 1975, and cited by the United Nations as a world model of conservation, are being quietly stripped away. It appears that the Harris government doesn't care about the incomparable and irreplaceable heritage of which future generations will be robbed.

The Chrétien government has adopted the same casual lack of concern about the even more critical future of the earth's atmosphere. It has broken its Red Book promises of environmental stewardship. The Prime Minister advised a United Nations meeting in June that "Canada, like most other industrialized countries, will not meet the year 2000 targets for stabilizing greenhouse gas emissions."[5]

Canada, one of the worst greenhouse polluters, agreed at Rio de Janeiro, in 1992, to stabilize greenhouse gas emissions at the 1990 levels. Instead we'll emit 8-13% more pollutants. Worse, our government has joined with the United States in blocking the future reductions that the European Union is seeking for the climate change conference to be held in Kyoto, Japan, in December 1997. Instead we support legally binding medium term targets but with no dates and no numbers.

One victim of the cutbacks brought my blood quickly to a boil. The federal government decided to slash the budget of the Fresh Water Institute by 70% even though fresh water lakes are one of Canada's most valuable resources. They are marvellous aides to rest and rehabilitation whether for the fisherman, dropping a hook in the water at twilight, or the swimmer, water-skier or canoeist. But the lakes have been under attack from acid rain and other forms of toxicity.

The Experimental Lakes Program, a child of the Institute, conducts research that is unique in the world. It uses real lakes to study fish habitat and the results are quite different from those of laboratory experiments. Live lakes are a luxury that few countries can afford but our abundance allowed us to blaze a trail and to become world leaders in a very important field of research.

When the public learned that the program would be decimated and the scientific team dispersed there were howls of protest. The government relented and reduced the cut from 70% to 40% which was enough to keep the project alive although many of the most experienced scientists are gone and new blood must be recruited.

THE ARTS

There are Canadians who feel that it is wrong to be concerned about the arts at a time when unemployment is high and welfare recipients are struggling to make ends meet. If it were really an either/or situation there would be merit in their case. But it isn't. With a common sense economic policy there would be room for progress on all fronts.

The arts are the soul of a nation, its self-expression, and there is no area in which Canada has made greater progress in the last half-century. It has been a matter of great pride to see fanciful ideas survive the pangs of birth, the struggling adolescence and finally achieve the adulthood of world class organizations. Les Feux Follet, of Montréal, the National and Royal Winnipeg Ballet companies, the Canadian Opera Company and the Shakespearean Festival in Stratford, which I have watched with enthusiasm since it was merely a gleam in Tom Patterson's eye, are but a few examples.

We have come a long way, especially since the Canada Council was born 40 years ago. It has helped the larger more established companies and, at the same time, also lent a helping hand to the smaller regional theatre companies, symphony orchestras, and talented individuals struggling to get a foot on the first rung of recognition. Not only have the arts flourished in Canada, they have become big business and an important tourist attraction, as well.

Recent years, however, have not been an easy time. Governments at all levels have cut support for the arts. Publishers have gone out of business, theatres have closed, and even the most respected organizations have been struggling to maintain their standards.

The artistic directors of the two organizations which I knew best departed Canada due to dreams unrealized. Lotfi Mansouri left the Canadian Opera Company when he concluded that plans for Toronto's Ballet Opera House would never be fulfilled. It was a great tragedy. The BOH, as it was known, was planned to be a world class facility. True, it would have been expensive but the reason for that was an immense back-stage — larger than the theatre itself — and a lot of high-tech machinery which would have allowed the National Ballet and the Canadian Opera Company to play in repertory. That meant a visitor from Rochester or Cleveland, with a weekend package tour, for example, would have had the choice of a ballet in the afternoon or an opera at night. Or both! The building was also designed with underground parking to provide the two companies with revenues equivalent to an endowment fund.

Now, years later, the Canadian Opera Company has plans to build an opera house on its own. The location is superb and I have no doubt that it will be grand in the best sense. But it will not have the extraordinary world class capacity for two companies to operate in repertory which would have brought visitors from the four corners of the earth to take a look. One more case of not stretching to our limits.

Reid Anderson, the Canadian-born artistic director of the National Ballet of Canada, decided to forsake his native land the night he learned that the Ontario Arts Council was reducing its grant by $426,000 which was 25% of the total. "After adjusting to one previous cut after another," he said, "it was the final straw."

Like most of Canada's arts companies both the National Ballet and the Canadian Opera Company are post-World War II phenomena. Their histories make fascinating reading. From extremely modest and tentative beginnings they both grew to achieve world class status. And while both are mature enough to survive the economic storm there has not been smooth sailing.

THE CBC

Not all Canadians love the CBC but many who do, love it with a passion. It has helped define who we are and what we are. It is a part of the Canadian psyche and has contributed much to the interpretation of one part of the country to another.

While most of us applauded the budgetary discipline which forced some belt-tightening, more recent cuts have forced the elimination of regional and other programming which is cutting to the core of the public broadcasting system. Canadianism is being squeezed in the direction of the lowest common denominator and the federal government has been derelict in cutting back to that extent.

SCIENCE AND TECHNOLOGY

We have also been short-changed in funds for scientific research. At a time when technology-based industries in other countries are growing at unprecedented speed, Canada cuts back. All the other G-7 countries have been boosting their budgets for technology and the emerging sciences where there is virtually unlimited potential for commercial benefit. In contrast Canada focuses on the past of budget deficits rather than the future of high-tech opportunity.

One must applaud the birth of the Canada Foundation for Innovation, announced in the 1997 budget, and the $180-million a year to modernize science, engineering, health and environmental research facilities and equipment. It will help to improve the infrastructure. But it is a hollow gesture without the funds for people and programs. Certainly business is providing more funds in some areas but always with strings attached. It is the responsibility of government to support the open-ended, no-strings-attached basic research fundamental to long-term scientific leadership.

THE ARMED FORCES

One of the current myths is that the malaise in the Canadian Armed Forces is directly attributable to the unification 30 years ago. This simply is not true as any scholarly review would find. Unification worked very well for the five years or so before it was overtaken by events. Morale was high, except for a few disgruntled senior officers, a wide variety of new equipment was being received and in the pipeline, the troops were well paid and their operational readiness was as good as it had been since the Korean War.

Unfortunately, in 1972, the government of the day decided to amalgamate the civil and military headquarters under the dual leadership of the Deputy Minister and the Chief of Defence Staff. The two-headed staff, comprised of both civilian and military officers, marked the beginning of what has been described as the "civilianization" of the armed forces. It was an unnatural mix of oil and water which could only lead to further irrational acts.

Those irrational acts lead to a piece-by-piece re-establishment of separate navy, army and air force headquarters, outside Ottawa, and the re-introduction of most of the waste, inefficiency and triplication of effort that unification had eliminated. Furthermore, the command structure became increasingly uncertain and confused. It became much more difficult to pinpoint responsibility.

It is something of a cop-out, however, to blame all the problems associated with leadership on the system — however bad. Honesty and integrity are character traits and there is no need to compromise them in a society which permits personal choice. Nor should it be assumed that a "cult of leadership" is exclusively a by-product of a particular form of organization. I can attest to a "cult of leadership" in the pre-unification days which, in the view of some, were the good old days.

While these things are difficult to prove, I would submit that 30 years of underfunding has been just as devastating to the efficiency and morale of the armed forces as the tangled web of organization. The present government cancelled the EH-101 helicopters for purely political reasons and is just now contemplating the purchase of an inferior model after having spent about half-a-billion in cancellation penalties. Worn-out submarines are not being replaced even though the British government offered to sell us some at bargain-basement prices. We have learned that troops were dispatched to Somalia without the equipment necessary to do the job. Obviously it would take years of substantially higher funding to bring all the forces' equipment up to an acceptable standard.

THE LIST GOES ON AND ON

Headline: Report warns of Toronto's decay. Poverty worsening, United Way says. Toronto's growing social problems have turned a clean-cut city into one perilously close to suffering the urban decay of big U.S. cities, Anne Golden, president of the United Way of Metropolitan Toronto warns.

"I can tell you honestly, when I read these statistics I feel we're seeing things before the downward spiral sets in," she said, after releasing a report that paints a bleak picture of social conditions in Toronto.[6]

Headline: Funding crisis threatens courts: McMurtry. Ontario's court system risks total breakdown unless the provincial government addresses a pressing need for more funding, the province's chief justice says. While "painful" budget cuts are necessary, the government must also realize that dollars spent on court staff, judges and courthouses will deliver big paybacks, including speedier trials.[7]

A few weeks earlier the Chief Justice of the Supreme Court of Canada, The Rt. Hon. Antonio Lamer, warned the federal government that any further cuts would seriously affect the operation of Canada's top court.

The fact is that our judicial system is already seriously overloaded. In August, 1997, for example, a Provincial Court Judge dismissed a charge of drug trafficking because the case was four years old. This may be justice for the accused but it doesn't make any sense for a society attempting to enforce socially acceptable standards of conduct.

Headline: Athletes take plea to Ottawa. Sprinter Donovan Bailey, unofficial spokesman for 90 Olympic and Paralympic athletes who were fêted in Ottawa, spoke forcefully about the need for greater government funding of the country's amateur athletes. "There has to be something done," said Bailey, "I was one of the struggling athletes at one time. I will always speak about it because I was there one time."[8]

Headline: Underfunded archive gets wallflower treatment. The National Archives of Canada is facing a 26 per cent cut over three years of its $58.3-million budget. As

Heather Robinson puts it, the feds treat the under-funded and neglected archives like "the smart girl in orthopedic shoes who never gets asked to dance."[9] Too true, and it's the heritage of our children and grandchildren that is being neglected.

STOP THE CARNAGE

These are examples of some of Canada's finest achievements which are being rapidly eroded. In each case it took years or decades to achieve a high standard of excellence. There is no physical reason why the pursuit of excellence could not have continued. The people were in place. They had the skills and organization necessary. Yet in each case their standards were under attack due to government cutbacks. The missing element in each case is money.

This leads me to a question that should be asked but seldom is. Why should great institutions be put in jeopardy when the only impediment to continued excellence is money? The blood, sweat and tears is available for the asking but money, which requires no comparable sacrifice, is not. So where is the problem?

Too many people think that there is just one jar full of money and when you run out there is no more. Not true! Money is a renewable resource which should be available in sufficient quantity to run the real economic machine that needs it. What is missing is the active participation of the Bank of Canada. It has abandoned the policy which enabled us to escape the Great Depression, finance the war and the prosperous post-war years. We must learn the lesson of history and use the bank creatively in the interest of all Canadians.

The inference of future chapters will be that it was not necessary to close one Canadian hospital; to raise university tuition fees; to cutback on environmental clean-up; to starve the armed forces of essential equipment; to cutback on money for the courts and, above all, to tolerate an immoral level of unemployment. These are all consequences of a phony economic "cult" from which we must free ourselves if we don't want to be totally engulfed by the evil empire.

CHAPTER 4

ABOUT MONEY

*"If the American people ever allow private banks to control
the issue of their currency, first by inflation and then
by deflation, the banks and the corporations that will
grow up around them will deprive the people of all
property until their children wake up homeless on
the continent their fathers conquered. "*

Thomas Jefferson

There would have been no need for Canada to abandon
its pursuit of excellence if our leaders had really understood the
"money game". It is indeed strange that so few people,
including the vast majority of politicians who spend so much
time talking about money, know so little about it. Adolescents
know where babies come from but only about one adult in every
hundred knows what money is and where it comes from. This
is not surprising when the educational system avoids the subject
as if it might lead to an outbreak of the plague.

Throughout history money has taken many forms with
the most predominant, until very recently, being coins of gold,
silver, copper and iron. The time came, however, when the
production of goods and services outstripped the happenstance
availability of precious metals and new forms of money had to
be invented.

In colonial days both British and French colonies in North America were desperately short of gold and silver money. As is always the case when there is too little money, commerce was affected negatively. In New France, which is now Canada, the French governor coped by cutting playing cards in four and signing them for use as money.

The British colonies began to print their own money. There is little doubt that the 13 American Colonies were the western pioneers in government-created money (GCM) — the kind that has sometimes been contemptuously labelled "funny money". Historians usually play down the role that this money-creation played in bringing about the U.S. War for Independence. It was Benjamin Franklin's view, however, that English restrictions on paper money constituted one of the main reasons for the alienation of the American provinces from the mother country. When the Continental Congress and the United States created large issues of their own legal tender money in 1775 it was so contrary to British law and so contemptuous of British sovereignty that war became inevitable.

The Americans won the war despite the British blockade and the deliberate attempt to discredit the Continental currency through counterfeiting. The Continental currency was discredited but the Colonies had the last laugh because they paid for much of the war effort with GCM. The total cost of the money borrowed, including interest, has been estimated at about $250-million until the debt was paid off. The British, on the other hand, relied heavily on bank-created borrowed money. In fact, according to William Hixson, in his excellent book *The Triumph of the Bankers*, the British taxpayers have paid over $4-billion in interest to their moneylending class of 1783 and its heirs over the last 200 years. And to add insult to injury, the original $500-million is still outstanding.[1]

While the Americans won the war, it is arguable that they lost the most important battle. As a result of the hyperinflation and discredited Continental currency, Alexander Hamilton was able to foist the British banking system on a reluctant America. He was bitterly opposed by Thomas Jefferson and his supporters but in the end Hamilton and the bankers prevailed, and the U.S. adopted the British fractional reserve system of banking. The argument as to which side was right has waged on and off for more than 200 years but the bankers have always won. It is noteworthy that Hamilton said, "A national debt, if it is not excessive, will be to us a national blessing." I have often wondered why he said that and what his reaction might be to the current $5-trillion U.S. federal debt.

THE FRACTIONAL RESERVE SYSTEM OF BANKING

When the fledgling Canadian Action Party's cartoon booklet describing the fractional reserve system of banking as a scam was distributed in the Atlantic provinces, two former bankers took umbrage. They found it impossible to believe that the system actually worked the way it was portrayed. The booklet raised issues that were new to them even though they had been involved in banking all their lives. In view of this sensitivity it might be better to call the system a "confidence game" although one of the former bankers insists that is no better than a scam. In any event, it is a system which only works as long as everyone has confidence that it will continue to work. When confidence is lost, as has happened from time to time, the system implodes.

Although European banking can be traced back to Roman times it is quite adequate for our purposes to begin this story with the London goldsmiths. Until 1640 it was the custom for wealthy merchants to deposit their excess cash — gold and silver — in the Mint of the Tower of London for safe-keeping. In that year Charles I seized the privately-owned money and destroyed the Mint's reputation as a safe place. This action forced merchants and traders to seek some other place to store their money. They opted for the goldsmiths of Lombard Street who already had strong fire-proof boxes for the storage of their own valuables.

The goldsmiths accepted deposits for which they issued receipts redeemable on demand. These receipts were passed from hand to hand and were known as goldsmith's notes, the predecessors of banknotes. The goldsmiths paid interest of 5 % on their customer's deposits and then lent the money to their more needy customers at exorbitant rates becoming, in fact, pawnbrokers who advanced money against the collateral of valuable property.[2] They also learned that it was possible to make loans in excess of the gold actually held in their vaults because only a small fraction of their depositors attempted to convert their receipts back into gold.

Thus began the fractional reserve system, the practice of lending "money" that doesn't really exist. It was to become the most profitable confidence game in the history of mankind. It was also the precedent on which the Bank of England was founded in 1694.

THE BANK OF ENGLAND LEGITIMIZED THE SCAM

The Bank of England was conceived as a solution to a dilemma. King William's War, 1688-1697, had been extremely costly and much of England's gold and silver had gone to the continent in payment for arms. As a result the money supply was sorely depleted and something had to be done to keep the wheels of commerce turning. It was decided that a bank might help to fill the void. So the Bank of England was chartered. The scheme involved an initial subscription by its shareholders of £1,200,000 in gold and silver which was lent to the government at 8 per cent. That was only the beginning, however, because in addition to a £4,000 management fee, the new Bank was granted authority to issue "banknotes" in an amount equal to its capital and lend the notes into circulation.

It was the same system developed by the goldsmiths. By lending the same money twice the Bank could double the interest received on its capital. Public acceptance of the banknotes was based on the assumption that they were "good as gold". Even when the Bank was subsequently authorized to increase the number of banknotes outstanding, in proportion to the gold in its vaults, the public seemed blithely unaware that the promise "to redeem in gold" was really a sham. The bankers got away with the deception because they knew, like the goldsmiths before them, that only a small fraction of banknote holders would attempt to redeem them at any one time. What had begun as a fraud had been legalized and legitimized, but that wasn't enough to protect the beneficiaries from the consequences of their own greed.

There were times when the Bank of England did not have enough gold in reserve to meet the day-to-day demands for conversion and within two years of operation an early "run" on the bank forced it to suspend payments in specie, that is, in coins as opposed to paper.[3] This was a situation that was to recur periodically through the next three centuries every time a "crisis" occurred as a result of a pressing need to increase the money supply at a rate in excess of the gold and silver reserves, or when banks got too greedy and put credibility to the test.

HIGHER LEVERAGE

In the slightly over 300 years since the Bank of England began with a leverage of two-to-one (twice interest on its capital) bank leverage has increased many times. In the early years of the 20th century federally chartered U.S. banks were required to have a gold reserve equal to 25% of deposits, that is banks could lend the same money four times. State chartered banks were subject to less restraint and there were some shocking examples of excess.

With the introduction of Central Banks, the Federal Reserve System in the U.S. and the Bank of Canada north of the border, the system changed in form though not in substance. Banknotes issued by private banks were phased out and replaced by a uniform, legal tender, currency. In the U.S., Federal Reserve Notes became predominant while in Canada the Bank of Canada was given a monopoly on the creation of legal tender paper money. In the process banks were no longer required to keep gold reserves against deposits but cash, legal tender, reserves instead.

Consequently in Canada, when I was younger, the cash reserve requirement for banks was 8% so they could lend the same money 12½ times. Today the cash reserve requirement in the U.S. is 3% for current accounts, 0% for savings accounts and 0% for Eurodollar accounts. In Canada, the reserve requirement is 0%, period. You are lucky if your bank has a cent, or a cent-and-a-half, for every dollar you think you have in the bank. The only reason they can get away with this is the time-honored one of knowing that only a handful of depositors are likely to ask for cash at any one time. If for any reason depositors' confidence was shaken and they began a "run" on the bank they would be out of luck in the absence of massive intervention by the Bank of Canada to monetize (print legal tender money to buy) the bank's bonds and other assets.

In lieu of cash reserves, Canadian banks are not allowed to own assets in excess of twenty times their paid up capital. It is a new system that the Bank for International Settlements (BIS) is trying to foist upon an unsuspecting world. It is part of the plan to switch the world banking system to 0% reserves in accord with Milton Friedman's latest canon.

Of Professor Friedman's several ideas none has greater potential for disaster than his support for deregulation of our financial institutions and getting governments out of the money-creation function. Accepting the notion of 0% cash reserves for deposit-taking institutions, thereby re-establishing private banks' virtual monopoly in the manufacture of money, will likely prove to be his greatest and most tragic legacy.

It is curious that Friedman would recommend 0% reserves when he claims to believe that 100% reserves, as recommended by his mentor, Lloyd W. Mints of the Chicago School of the 1930s, would be better.[4] His only explanation for jumping from 100% to 0% is politics. He has concluded that establishing a 100% reserve system is politically impossible whereas the adoption of the 0% reserve system is politically feasible. He is right on that score as Canada has led the way in letting the banks get away with 0% reserves.

In addition to putting the money-creation function almost entirely in private hands, which history has demonstrated to be an unworkable system, it has the additional disadvantage of being a "risk-weighted" system. Under the BIS formula, adopted by the Canadian Parliament, it is more advantageous for banks to buy government bonds than it is to make commercial loans.   This is because business loans are considered "risky", and consequently must be backed by 8% of the banks' capital compared to a maximum of 5% for government bonds which are considered risk free — a dubious assumption for some OECD countries' bonds.   Once again it is the real, wealth-creating economy that suffers.

Apart from the utter hopelessness of a money-creation system based entirely on debt, high bank leverage has been the endemic weakness of the capitalist system.   When times are good we allow the banks to blow up the money supply like a balloon.   Then if inflation results and central banks want to tighten the money supply the leverage works in reverse — like a balloon with a pin stuck in it.   It is no accident that there have been 45 recessions and depressions in the last 200 years.   In my opinion every one of them had its origin in the fractional reserve banking system.

BANKS PRINT MONEY

I use the word "print" for the benefit of the media who appear to have a hang-up about it.   I could just have easily used words like "create" or "manufacture".   It's all the same.   The first Governor of the Bank of Canada, Graham Towers, said that banks manufacture money as steel companies manufacture steel.   That is their business.   Towers also said that Parliament could change the system if it wanted to.

Bankers usually insist that they are simply financial intermediaries and that they only lend their depositors' money.   It is true that they are financial intermediaries and lend depositors' money but that isn't all.   They also create new money every time they make a new loan — or destroy money if they cancel one.   The system works this way.

A builder needs to borrow $150,000 to build a house.   Once sufficient collateral has been agreed upon with the bank, a note will be signed and, presto, $150,000 is put in the builder's account.   The important point is that just minutes earlier the $150,000 didn't exist.   It was created out of thin air based on nothing more than a small capital reserve as required by the Bank Act.

The money is then used to pay the people who dig clay from a pit and make bricks, the bricklayers who lay the bricks, the woodsmen who cut trees to make lumber, the carpenters who use it to build the frame, the miners who extract the metals for the hardware and the manufacturers who turn out the plumbing, wiring and fixtures. But when they are all finished it is the bank which owns the house.

All the bank did was create the "money" which acted as the intermediary to facilitate construction. Nevertheless, because it was created as debt, all of the new money used to pay for the new house has a lien on it. Consequently the builder has to sell the house at a price that will allow him to repay the bank and, if he is lucky, leave a little over to reward him for the work he has done and the risk he has taken. If he can't, and there is a shortfall, he will have to make up the difference to prevent the bank from liquidating part or all of the collateral pledged to get the loan.

In reality, then, the banks have turned the world into one gargantuan pawn shop. You hock your stocks, bonds, house, business, rich mother-in-law or country and the bank(s) will create a loan based on the value of the collateral. At least that is the way it has been. If you look at bank reports today you see that they are converting to giant casinos as they play with stocks, bonds, options, currencies and derivatives, often with uncertain risk. It is not a system designed for quiet sleep.

A FAULTY SYSTEM

There are several fundamental faults in a system where privately-owned banks create all or nearly all of the new money created each year. One is the historic instability already discussed. It is a boom-bust system which led to socialism, communism and fascism as economic distress provided a fertile ground for leaders promising a better system.

A by-product of the instability is the waste. Every time the cycle turns down, human and economic resources are sacrificed. In a system geared to debt, an economy can only expand when someone — business, individuals or governments — is prepared to borrow more and go deeper in debt. That's the only way the money supply will increase and the economy grow. Steady growth demands that consumers, business and governments, all three, are willing to increase their debt load. When one or more of the partners is unable or unwilling to increase their debt load, as has been the case in Canada in recent years, the economy stagnates.

Finally, and most important of all, a system of privately-created money is not sustainable. The only reason the system worked in the early post-World War II years is because the money-creation function was shared with government. The Bank of Canada provided the federal government with significant sums of near-zero interest money which gave it some fiscal flexibility. In addition, interest rates in the '50s and '60s were below the growth rate of the economy. Consequently total debt grew in proportion to the economy but the debt to GDP ratio didn't increase.

All that changed with the adoption of monetarism and floating interest rates. Interest rates are far higher now, about double the growth rate of the economy, so the debt is compounding, the debt to GDP ratio is skyrocketing, and we are headed for a massive "correction" in the absence of an equally massive dose of common sense.

GOVERNMENT-CREATED MONEY IS ESSENTIAL!

It should be patently clear by now that a system under which all new money is created by private corporations as debt is not a sustainable system. We learned that lesson in the late 1920s and 1930s but seem to have forgotten it. A highly leveraged banking system aided and abetted the stock market boom of 1929. The crash brought a substantial collapse of bank-created credit money and with it the worst depression ever, so far.

It took the infusion of significant amounts of government-created money and a war to get us out of the slump. GCM helped finance the war and lay the foundation for the best 25 years Western capitalism has ever known. So we have to learn the lesson of history and get government back into the money-creation business for three important reasons: (a) greater stability in the banking system, (b) more fiscal flexibility for government to facilitate lower unemployment by permitting the funding of useful investments in the economy, and (c) as the only means of putting a cap on the total debt to GDP ratio.

THE MEANS

There have been cases, as in the United States, where the federal treasury printed money on its own behalf. More recently, however, governments have relied on the facility of their central banks. In Canada, the Bank of Canada, bought Government of Canada bonds with funds created for that purpose.

This is the system that was in effect from the 1930s until 1974. It worked quite well and, in addition to providing the government with fiscal flexibility, saved taxpayers a lot of money. It is much cheaper to borrow from your own bank at 0% interest than from the chartered banks at 6 per cent.

This system would work well for refinancing government debt and reducing the cost of servicing the debt. As bonds come due the Bank of Canada could buy a substantial portion of the new issue. That way it could rebuild its share of federal debt and save taxpayers billions in the process.

The technique of buying bonds would be less satisfactory if we decided that 50% of all new money should be government-created. Assume that the amount of money put into circulation might average $30-billion a year for five years, until unemployment is brought down to the 4%-5% range, and that half of the new money was GCM. In 5 years the total of government bonds outstanding would increase by $75-billion — from about $600-billion to $675-billion. While the increase would be meaningless in that we would owe it to ourselves, many people find difficulty in differentiating between government debt held by the public and government debt held by the central bank. Consequently the "debt clocks" that the Vancouver Board of Trade and the Toronto Sun have on their walls to warn of an impending crisis would show a constant increase. Under those circumstances it would be difficult to persuade people that the perception was not reality.

AN ALTERNATE APPROACH

One solution is to have the Treasury print its own money. There is precedent for that in both Canada and the U.S. This would appear to be retrograde today, however, when both countries rely on central banks for the day-to-day control of the money supply to the extent that such control is possible. Working through them would be more acceptable than setting up a parallel system.

The alternative I have suggested is that the Treasury sell shares in Canada to the Bank of Canada for $1-billion each. The shares would not be transferable under any circumstances. They would be, in effect, simply an accounting device, and nothing more. The way the Bank of Canada operates, it has to have an asset on its books equivalent to the cash it creates which is booked as a liability. (Don't ask me why cash is created as a liability when it can't be redeemed in anything except equivalent cash. It is one of those imponderables like Santa Claus and the tooth fairy which just have to be accepted.) The shares would provide the essential asset for accounting purposes.

Putting money into circulation in exchange for shares is the best way to cap the total debt to GDP ratio. It would truly be interest-free money and would be a counterbalance to some of the interest on existing debt. This method would also have the previously stated advantage of providing more stability for the banking system while providing greater fiscal flexibility for government. As with the previous system of creating cash for bonds it would be essential to reinstate reserve requirements for deposit-taking institutions and to increase the reserve requirement proportional to the cash created.

HOW MUCH GCM IS ENOUGH?

That is a moot point. The Chicago School of the 1930s, and Yale Professor Irving Fisher, believed that government should create all of the new money created each year. That would mean that all bank deposits would be backed by 100% cash. This is also the view Milton Friedman cites as his preferred position but one he believes to be politically impossible.

In my two books on the subject I suggested a GCM/BCM split of 50/50 for all new money created. That would be less of a shock for the banking system and one that would allow it to adjust without too much difficulty — a gentle increase of about 2-2½% a year in cash reserve requirements. This is my preferred position although I may have to re-consider if the trend to globalization continues unabated. In that event it might be necessary for each country to create all of its own currency in order to survive as independent entities. The banks, then, would be restricted to financial intermediation.

Any amount of GCM is going to require a considerable amount of public education. In the June '97 federal election campaign the Canadian Action Party proposed the infusion into the Canadian economy of $10-billion GCM which would have been enough to reinstate all of the most important federal and provincial programs that had fallen victim to the deficit reduction program. A number of uninformed wiseacres said the program would be inflationary. Not so! Printing the money to pay a few nurses, teachers and scientists about to be fired would not be inflationary. It would only be inflationary if there were comparable jobs readily available for them to go to and you started bidding up salaries in the process.

The truth is that the $10-billion infusion we proposed is almost exactly the amount of money that will be extinguished in 1997 as a result of bankruptcies. With so many people unemployed and so much unused capacity in the economy, $10-billion would not have had any measurable influence on prices. The figure is about 50% of what the private banks created last year which was not enough to finance an acceptable rate of growth.   It appears the banks will create substantially more credit money in 1997 as low interest rates encourage consumers to assume more debt.

Any orthodox economist will agree that it is the total amount of money created that affects prices, not who creates it. The difference between BCM and GCM is that one puts the system into an ever widening circle of debt while the other tends to slow the spiral and provide debt relief.

— — —

N.B.   For a more comprehensive discussion of the subject of money, what it is and where it comes from please read one or more of the books listed in the back after the notes.

CHAPTER 5

A DISASTROUS BANK OF CANADA

"O wad some Pow'r the giftie gie us to see oursels
as others see us. "

Robert Burns

The banking system played a key role in the "golden years" we enjoyed in the 1950s and 1960s. It has played an equally critical role in the downturn of our fortunes which began in the 1970s. Therefore, it is worthwhile to review some of the changes in the Bank of Canada's policies and to take a look at the expansion of power and influence by the privately-owned chartered banks.

The Bank of Canada was born in 1934 with great expectations. It was the depth of the Great Depression and ordinary people hoped that it would mitigate the boom-bust cycle which had been so much a part of capitalism. The chartered banks, as might be expected, opposed the move because they didn't want anyone interfering with their monopoly to print money. Eventually they accepted the inevitable and began the never-ending process of attempting to divert the central banks policies away from the public interest in favor of their own.

Originally the Bank of Canada was privately-owned but, in 1938, it was nationalized by Prime Minister W.L. Mackenzie King in fulfillment of one of his 1935 election promises. It was then perfectly positioned to play a key role in helping Canada escape the Great Depression and finance World War II. It did this by creating (printing) money for the benefit of the government of Canada.

The money created by the Bank of Canada for the federal government was, to all intents and purposes, interest-free. This government-created money (GCM), printed by the Bank of Canada, was used to buy Government of Canada bonds. The government paid interest on the bonds which was then returned to the government as dividends with only the Bank of Canada's day-to-day operating expenses being deducted. So the cost of the money was less than 1 per cent. In addition, the cash printed by the Bank of Canada, when spent into circulation by the government, wound up in the private banks where it became the base for a rapid expansion of bank-created money (BCM). When the private banks created money to buy government bonds, however, the interest paid by the government accrued to the banks.

At least with the advent of the Bank of Canada the money-creation function was shared between the government and the private banks. This improved arrangement provided the Government of Canada with some fiscal flexibility that it hadn't enjoyed previously. This was useful in wartime and afterward to help finance the roads, bridges, airports, and social programs that made Canada great.

The post-war years were a period when the Bank of Canada performed quite well. It deliberately kept interest rates low which reduced the carrying charges on the wartime debt to a minimum. Low interest rates also encouraged rapid economic growth so the Gross Domestic Product increased by an average 5.04% from 1948 to 1973. The combination of rapid growth and low interest rates allowed the economy to expand at about the same rate as the total debt while the ratio of federal debt to GDP declined dramatically. These were indeed the "golden years".

THE BANK FOR INTERNATIONAL SETTLEMENTS

In 1974, when Gerald Bouey was Governor, the Bank of Canada changed course and adopted monetarism as official policy. This was the worst decision in the history of the Bank and whether it was Bouey's idea or whether it originated with the Bank for International Settlements (BIS) we may never know.

The governors of the industrialized world's central banks and the chairman of the U.S. Federal Reserve Board meet regularly, in secret, at the headquarters of the Bank for International Settlements in Basel, Switzerland. It has all the trappings of a conclave of bishops and is so secret that not even ministers of finance are allowed to attend. It is alleged that the adoption of monetarism as holy writ was a collegial decision. Whether true or not, the policy switch of central banks including the Bank of Canada can be pretty well traced to that date.

Governor Bouey gave us a tentative trial run in 1974-75 when he induced a minor recession. It was a foretaste of things to come. Government revenues did not increase as fast as previously projected. Consequently the deficit almost tripled from about $2¼-billion to a little over $6-billion and the net public debt jumped from about $28½-billion to just over $34½-billion, by far the largest year over year increase since World War II.

It was, however, merely a warm-up for the main event scheduled for 1981-82. By then President Jimmy Carter's nominee Paul Volcker had become Chairman of the Federal Reserve Board (FED) in the United States, and he was a disciple of Friedmanism to the n'th degree. In 1979 he began tinkering with the U.S. money supply with weird and unpredicted results but he decided to stay the course and put monetarism to the ultimate test, squeezing inflation out of the U.S. economy totally.

The FED squeezed the system as it had never been deliberately squeezed before. Other central banks, including the Bank of Canada, with Bouey at the helm, did likewise.

Interest rates moved to historic highs as the growth of Western economies came shuddering to a halt. Millions of innocent people lost their jobs. Hundreds of thousands of others lost their homes when they couldn't afford to pay the high interest rates. Tens of thousands more lost their farms, often after several generations in the family, and businesses went bankrupt on a scale unseen since the onslaught of the Great Depression — all victims of the most cold-hearted and inhumane economic manoeuvre in human history.

FIRST PRIZE FOR STUPIDITY

When you stop to think about it can you think of anything more stupid than this? One branch of government, the Bank of Canada, deliberately and callously puts half a million people out of work. Then other branches of that same government start scrambling around trying to dream up new programs designed to put a few of the same people back to work. Can you think of any greater insanity?

In the June 1982 and April 1983 federal budgets, hundreds of millions of additional dollars were allocated to the Canada Community Development Program, the Enterprise Development Program, the Defence Industries Productivity Program, Regional Industrial Expansion Program, special youth programs and many other job-creation initiatives. The result was more spending and a bigger deficit leading to more debt. Naturally the politicians were blamed for responding to public pressure to repair some of the damage caused by the Bank of Canada's tight money, high interest rate policy.

It is an interesting footnote that, notwithstanding the carnage, and with Western economies looking as if they were blitzed by atomic bombs, monetarism was not put to the ultimate test of eliminating inflation completely because Volcker and the others realized, just in time, that if they didn't turn off their death machines the whole Western monetary system would collapse. In that case there would have been an implosion unlike anything the world had ever seen before. It would have made the Great Depression look like a Sunday School picnic.

THE CONSEQUENCE OF EVIL IS DEBT

Still, the damage that had already been done was beyond calculation. The human suffering and distress cannot be described in words — careers destroyed, families broken up, hopes and dreams dashed. Nor can the economic fall-out be adequately measured. The 1981-82 recession resulted in government revenues remaining flat — billions less than projected. Program spending had to be increased to alleviate the suffering. The federal deficit took the biggest one year jump ever from just over $15½-billion to $29-billion and, thanks to high interest rates, the net public debt followed suit rising from about $107½-billion to $136½-billion.

The data for federal debt to GDP ratios in both the U.S. and Canada make it painfully clear that the current debt crises had their origin in the recession of 1981-82. Indeed Statistics Canada prepared a study which reached this conclusion but was asked by the Department of Finance to withdraw it because the facts were out of harmony with the "party line".

It could be suggested here that central banks had no alternative, but that simply is not true. A simple, painless incomes policy like the one I have been promoting for almost 30 years (about which more will be said later) would not have reduced government revenues, would not have increased unemployment and would not have resulted in either increased deficit or debt. Furthermore, inflation would have been wrestled to the ground to a greater extent than that achieved by the horrendous recession. But incomes policies were an anathema to monetarism which insisted on its own blunt high interest rate approach. It only partially succeeded in getting the inflation genie back in the bottle while releasing the debt genie to plague us for generations to come.

FROM WORSE TO WORST

The accession of John Crow to the Governor's throne corresponded with Canada's worst era of monetary management. We had not yet recovered from the damaging blow inflicted by Mr. Bouey's 1981-82 recession when John Crow decided to give it to us again on the other cheek in 1990. A monetarist ideologue, he even beat the U.S. with his timing of the nasty punch. Our recession and the subsequent period of slow growth began before theirs and lasted longer — so long, in fact, that Professor Pierre Fortin, of the Université de Québec à Montreàl, labelled it the "Great Canadian Slump".

Even some monetarists, or neo-classical economists as they are beginning to call themselves now that pure monetarism has been widely discredited, believe that Crow overshot the mark with his ultimate aim of zero inflation. Not even the U.S. went that far and the different targets are credited with the different unemployment rates in the two countries — the U.S. 5% rate being little more than half of our 9 per cent.

In any event, the results of Crow's excess have been disastrous. In the aftermath of the 1990 and subsequent squeeze federal government revenues actually fell from $122- billion in '91-'92 to about $116-billion in '93-'94. Taxes, which were already too high, had to be increased to compensate. The federal deficit, which had dropped from $38.4-billion in '84-'85 to $28.9-billion in '89-'90, took off again to reach a high of $42-billion in '93-'94. Needless to say the debt continued to sky-rocket.

CROW TO GO?

I thought that John Crow was such an unmitigated disaster as Governor that I did everything I could think of to have him replaced. I wrote a letter to all Liberal Members of Parliament suggesting they introduce a Bill in the House declaring the office of the Governor to be vacant. This is the only way a Governor can be removed before his term of office expires. I knew that most Conservative back-benchers wanted to see Crow go and I suspected the same was true of the Liberals. A trip to Ottawa where I chatted with several MPs confirmed the sentiment and I hoped for some action but no one was brave enough to act. Some of the letters, explaining the inaction, were masterpieces of subterfuge.

I also took the case directly to Prime Minister Brian Mulroney. From experience I knew the only way to ensure that he saw a letter was to hand it to him personally. So I attended the unveiling of a statue to Mike Pearson where I knew Brian would be attending and handed it to him as he left. But not before the sharp edge of a Mountie's hand racked my other one as I held out the envelope. It was the first and only occasion on which a policeman has "laid a hand on me."

When the prime minister turned to say hello and take the envelope, all was well. I knew he would read it, which he subsequently confirmed. It said, in brief, that Crow's high interest rate and high Canadian dollar policies were having a devastating effect; he should bring Derek Burney, our Ambassador to the U.S., back to Ottawa; send Finance Minister Mike Wilson to Washington to replace Burney and get a new finance minister to order Crow to reduce interest rates ¼ % a month until they reached an acceptable level. If he refused, replace him. Also, back away from the Goods and Services Tax (GST) which was being introduced at the worst possible time.

Months later he phoned me and said he had just re-read the letter. Obviously he was troubled by the policy choices confronting him. He started telling me about all the tough decisions his government was making — "not political, but in the long-term interests of the country." Finally, I asked him to cut the baloney; he was talking to me and not making a stump speech. We chatted for 20 minutes and I could hear the wheels turning. A few days later he announced the appointment of eight extra senators to force through the passage of the GST and I knew that, once again, the bureaucrats had won over common sense.

After the election of November 1993, during which the Liberals promised to get rid of the GST, they finally decided not to reappoint Crow. A few well placed telephone calls resulted in spate of columns and letters to the editor demanding that Crow must go. The public response was swift and unequivocal. Crow was not reappointed for a second term. Instead he was replaced with a more congenial clone.

MORE OF THE SAME

When Gordon Thiessen took the helm from John Crow, he and finance minister Paul Martin agreed that there would be no change in the Bank of Canada's 1% to 3% target range for inflation. Tight money and high interest rates would continue, notwithstanding the unconscionably high unemployment rate in the 9% to 10% range.

As the government reached the second half of its mandate, however, and it appeared that the moribund state of the economy might contribute to its defeat, the Bank of Canada did the first smart thing it had done in years — it reduced interest rates steadily and significantly until the Bank's discount rate fell below that of the FED in the U.S.

There is no doubt of the wisdom of this move except for the fact that it should have been done years sooner. The low interest rates finally sparked a modest recovery in the summer of 1997. The kindest thing that one can say is, "better late than never." The anticipated growth rate of up to 4% in 1997 and 3% in 1998 is high by recent standards but still not high enough to bring unemployment down to morally acceptable levels. That would require a growth rate of 4½% to 5% for four or five years which not even the optimists are forecasting. The goal should be to reduce unemployment by at least 1% a year until it hits 4 per cent.

One thing the recent decline in interest rates has proved is that Canadian interest rates can be as low or lower than those in the United States as long as our inflation rate is significantly lower than the one south of the border. This was a hypothesis put forward years ago by those of us who favored an incomes policy to control inflation but the idea was usually rejected by mainline economists. Now, at long last, it has been proven and it's about time.

IS THE GOOD NEWS TEMPORARY?

There are two aspects of Bank of Canada policy which keep us in a state of nervous uncertainty. The first is Governor

Thiessen's unwritten determination to keep the Canadian dollar from falling far below the 72-cent range. When it dropped to 71.63-cents he raised the discount rate by ¼ per cent. And financial markets are counting on him to do it again if the dollar comes under pressure.

There is no proof that propping up the Canadian dollar in this way is in Canada's best interests. All it does is export jobs by subsidizing imports and increase the deficit by making it more expensive to service the national debt. It is also bad for tourism which is one of Canada's most important industries. It is just recovering from John Crow's high dollar policy and doesn't need another setback. These important disadvantages outweigh any obvious advantage of keeping the exchange rate within a narrow band.

The second aspect is even more fundamental. As part of its monetarist theology, the Bank of Canada has adopted the notion of a "natural rate of unemployment" which is sometimes referred to as the nonaccelerating inflation rate of unemployment (NAIRU). Of all the jargon invented by monetarists to justify the inhumanity of their system none is more worrisome. Even Milton Friedman who invented the term "natural rate of unemployment" is at a loss to explain what it is. And since you can't put a number on it, it moves up and down to accommodate other economic circumstances, which proves there is nothing "natural" about it at all. Still, the idea hangs over the Canadian economy like a Sword of Damocles.

There are three necessary conditions if the Canadian economy is to operate in the best interest of all Canadians in the years ahead. These are low interest rates, a low dollar and low unemployment. Governor Thiessen has made it very clear, however, that we can expect none of these. On October 1, 1997, after only three months of reasonable growth, he raised interest rates by ¼ per cent. He has also warned that further increases are in store — the antithesis of what Canada really needs.[1] All this with no serious public discussion or debate and certainly without the sanction or approval of Parliament. The Bank of Canada has become a law unto itself — a situation which no responsible government should tolerate.

THE PITS AS MONEY MANAGERS

One of the Bank of Canada's functions is to manage the federal government's debt and borrowing. In this capacity it has been an abject failure. One would expect its mandate would be to minimize the federal debt. Instead, they have maximized it. As already pointed out, Canada's public debt is, for the most part, a direct result of the 1981-82 and 1990-91 recessions. The deficits caused by the recessions were rolled over into debt and then compounded with extraordinarily and unnecessarily high interest rates.

Furthermore, the Bank of Canada even stopped doing its fair share of financing the debt with government-created money. In 1974 the Bank of Canada held more than 20% of Canadian government debt. This, as I explained earlier, was the equivalent of an interest-free loan. But in accordance with monetarist dogma it began to reduce its share until today it only holds about 5% of government debt. This change in policy — which once again was never explained or debated — has cost Canadian taxpayers more than $90-billion in interest and interest on the interest.

Worse, when it ceased buying its fair share of bonds the Bank felt it necessary to increase interest rates to encourage (bribe) foreigners to buy the bonds it was not buying. The higher interest rates increased our debt service charges and put us deeper in hock both domestically and internationally.

Finally, by increasing interest rates ¼% on October 1, 1997, and telegraphing further increases to come, it increased the rate necessary for the 1997 Series, Canada Savings Bonds. Any private money managers with such a dismal record would be instantly fired.

LIES AND DAMN LIES

Among the lies that Bank of Canada governors have perpetrated by innuendo is that the huge government debt is due to program overspending including health-care and social services. Much worse, they have persuaded an uncritical press and an uninformed public to believe them.

If they had said that some waste and extravagance had crept into these programs they would have been right. But to blame the $600-billion debt on overspending is grossly misleading. As Chart 1 shows, of the $561-billion increase in the public debt from 1946-1996 only slightly over $15-billion, a little less than 3%, is directly due to program spending. The balance, more than 97%, is due to compound interest.

CHART 1

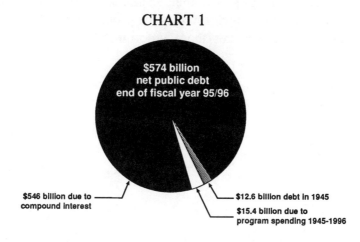

$546 billion due to compound interest

$574 billion net public debt end of fiscal year 95/96

$12.6 billion debt in 1945

$15.4 billion due to program spending 1945-1996

Sources: Public Accounts of Canada, 1995-96 and Department of Finance

THE BOTTOM LINE

The bottom line is that the performance of the Bank of Canada since 1974 has been one of total disaster. It has been primarily responsible for the slow growth economy. Governor Thiessen's speeches plugged cutbacks in government spending in order to reduce the deficit.[2] He didn't even allude to the alternative policy of operating the economy at its full potential with full employment which would have been both a faster and more humane way of reducing the deficit and balancing the budget. From 1974 to date the Canadian economy has underperformed by hundreds of billions of dollars. The Bank of Canada put a governor on Canada's economic car so we could never get it going faster than low or second gear.

The slow growth — and for a while no growth — economy with its recessions and high interest rates is primarily responsible for the deficits, debt and crippling unemployment. It has dug us into a hole so deep that there is no orthodox escape. It has been a crime against humanity and if there were any real justice, Messrs. Bouey, Crow and Thiessen would all be in jail instead of the many people who have been driven to crime by the desperation of their economic circumstances. But our system is one which rewards the people who make hurtful decisions and penalizes those unfortunates who suffer as a result.

CHAPTER 6

THE BANKS PLAY MONOPOLY

"Banking was conceived in iniquity and was born in sin. The Bankers own the earth. Take it away from them, but leave them the power to create money, and with a flick of the pen they will create enough money to buy it back again. However, take that power away from them and all the great fortunes like mine will disappear, and they ought to disappear, for this would be a happier and better world to live in. But if you wish to remain the slaves of Bankers, and pay the cost of your own slavery, let them continue to create money. "

Sir Josiah Stamp, Director, Bank of England[1]

Banks are unique amongst commercial institutions in that they are the only corporations with licenses to print money. They don't actually print banknotes, as they did before the Bank of Canada was given a monopoly in 1935 to print the kind of money we carry in our pocketbooks and purses. Today the new money is created by the chartered banks — and they create a lot of it as we will see in a later chapter — by using a computer.

The patent for the creation of new money is owned by the federal Parliament on behalf of the Canadian people. But for reasons which have much more to do with historical precedent than any kind of logic, Parliament has licensed its patent to the commercial banks. The licenses are called bank charters issued under the authority of the Bank Act. The charters are renewed each time the Bank Act is renewed — usually about every five years.

To the extent that there is any logic in allowing banks to create money, it is that they will ration the money more fairly and wisely than government would. Their branch managers have been well positioned to get to know the farmers, business people and small entrepreneurs in need of financial assistance and to determine their creditworthiness.

A case can be made that the system made some sense, although the banks were often unreasonable in their demands for collateral and merciless in their treatment of borrowers in default. It began to make less sense when banks got tired of the work involved in servicing their small customers, the ones who create the jobs, and turned their attention to wholesale, large-loan banking — including buyouts which resulted in bidding up the price of assets (causing inflation) and then the elimination of redundant personnel (adding to unemployment).

This shift in strategy by the banks seriously undermined the public trust aspect of their charters. Deals that were profitable to them were often contrary to the public interest. Wholesale banking also introduced a double standard. Loans to high-flying real estate operators were not collateralized to the extent small business loans had been. Furthermore, loans to Third World countries were not collateralized at all. So the banks' ability to act fairly and wisely, implicit in their charters, was exposed as largely myth.

Where the logic of Parliament allowing private corporations to create money breaks down completely is when the federal government allows the banks to print money to buy federal bonds and then acts as a collection agency for the banks to make sure we pay the interest on that money — perhaps in perpetuity, if the present system persists. It would be a little less painful if Parliament imposed a healthy royalty for the use of its money-creation patent. But the license, which has to be the most lucrative of all monetary windfalls, is issued without a royalty provision! Worse, the federal government, which still has the right to use its own patent, but which stubbornly refuses to use this valuable asset in its own best interests, pays handsomely for the periodic use of the licenses it has issued and lines up meekly at the banks like a sheep at the shearers.

SPREADING THE NET

You would think that when the banks have such a good thing going for them that they would be content. But that is not the case. Every time the Bank Act is reviewed, and their charters renewed, they ask for more. Profitability is the name of the game and each time they extend their tentacles into other people's businesses, competition is reduced and the banks relentless drive toward monopolizing the financial sector advances one step further.

At one time there were "four pillars" of the financial world — banks, trust, securities and insurance companies. The banks have effectively bulldozed two of the other three pillars, trust companies and securities dealers, to the point where the few remaining independents are the notable exceptions. They are now working on the fourth pillar, the insurance companies, and only an unmistakable government vote of disapproval will prevent the near total consolidation of the financial services industry under the banks' umbrella.

To accomplish their ends the banks have used every tactic and argument their high-priced talent could dream up. A few years ago, when the banks were not allowed to make consumer loans, the Bank of Nova Scotia began to defy the law while counting on its propaganda offensive to the effect that it would save consumers money. The gamble paid off, the restriction on consumer loans was lifted. Most of the consumer loan companies disappeared.

When Jacques Parizeau, then finance minister in the Liberal government in Québec, decided to play Québec interests against those of Ontario by allowing provincially chartered deposit-taking institutions to buy into brokerage firms he set off a chain of events which he did not envisage. The threat of losing business was the wedge needed to pry loose more favorable regulations from Ontario regulators who dropped the rule limiting banks to 10% ownership of a brokerage firm.

The Toronto-Dominion Bank provided the thin edge of the wedge with its Green Line Service which was restricted at the outset but was soon liberated as the barriers fell and the race

was on. Royal Bank bought Dominion Securities, the Bank of
Montreal bought Nesbitt Thomson, the CIBC bought Wood
Gundy, the Bank of Nova Scotia acquired McLeod Young Weir
and the National Bank swallowed Levésque-Beaubien, the
largest Québec-based dealer.

These takeovers constituted one of the biggest
consolidations of power and influence in the history of
Canadians financial institutions. It also posed a new dilemma
for banks owning a broker. How could it deal at arms length
with its subsidiary which was borrowing money to buy stocks
or to float new share issues? And would it be influenced in any
way in making credit available to customers wishing to buy
shares being peddled by a subsidiary?

The answer, we were told, was Chinese walls. One
branch of the conglomerate would be forbidden to whisper, let
alone to speak of, information that would be of advantage or
disadvantage to its subsidiary and this prohibition would apply
in both directions.

It was the joke of the century. Within weeks of the ink
being dry on the Royal Bank takeover of Dominion Securities
I had a call from a retail salesperson. The Royal Bank
Quarterly Statement would be coming out in a few days, I was
informed. The results would be excellent and it was anticipated
that the market value of Royal Bank stock would rise. I was
appalled that the myth of inter-branch secrecy would be stripped
bare so quickly. As a matter of principle I didn't buy any
Royal Bank stock but any moral gain was at a financial cost
because the results were good and the price did go up.

THE COUP OF 1991

The banks were not satisfied with gobbling up most of
the major securities dealers. They wanted more. So in advance
of the 1991 revisions of the Bank Act they lobbied ferociously
in favor of the idea of "one-stop financial shopping" under
which, presumably, anyone in the financial services business
could own anything. Equally insidious, they argued that the
trust companies had an advantage because they were not

required to maintain cash reserves against their deposits (about which more will be said later). What they wanted was a "level playing field".

That sounds like a "tilt" if ever I heard one. There is no such thing as a level playing field when you are playing against the banks. It is interesting that the banks didn't argue that the trust companies and other deposit-taking institutions should be required to maintain cash reserves. The banks wanted them eliminated altogether after re-naming them a "tax on the banks".

Well, it must have been Christmas in bankland. Brian Mulroney's finance minister, Michael Wilson, introduced a bill removing the rules that kept the banks from majority ownership of trust companies and out of the insurance game. They were not allowed to sell insurance over the counter in their branches but they were allowed to buy trust and insurance companies.

Another pot of gold was the total elimination, over a three-year period, of the cash reserve requirement. This bonanza was worth billions to the banks and while the whole gift package was being wrapped in legislative cellophane with a pretty ribbon and the bow tied, members of Parliament slept. This is not surprising for government backbenchers who open their mouths at considerable risk; but one wonders what kind of gas was required to muzzle the Liberal opposition to such a degree that one would have thought that they were in a state of winter hibernation.

The removal of statutory reserve requirements effective July 1994 provided an incentive for the banks to reduce their note holdings. The proportion of currency (GCM) in circulation held by chartered banks has thus declined from nearly 17% in 1991 to less than 11% in 1996.[2] The reduced need for cash — the banks truck it back and forth between branches overnight in order to keep inventories low — means less seigniorage for the Crown. One more way of diverting money from the public coffers to bank tills. Even federal officials are concerned that the explosive increase in the use of credit cards, debit cards and cash cards will mean an even further loss of seigniorage.

You have already guessed the banks' next move in this decades long monopoly game. They rescued the struggling trust companies, whose earlier advantage they considered so unfair, by buying them. In doing so they virtually eliminated the modest competition the trust companies had provided with their longer hours, marginally higher interest rates paid on deposits, split level mortgages and flexible Guaranteed Investment certificates. Today, following the purchase of National Trust by the Bank of Nova Scotia, there is only one large independent trust company remaining, Canada Trust. There are rumours that the Canadian Imperial Bank of Commerce would like to buy it some propitious day when the government thinks the press and public will not take too much notice.

The impact of all this consolidation is almost beyond comprehension. Slowly but surely the banks have been getting into other people's businesses. First they infiltrate, like the camel getting its head into the tent, and then they take over. The big six now own more than 400 subsidiaries and the list is growing. In addition to financial services they are now involved in energy, aviation, leasing, insurance and other activities.

Their success is reflected in their enormous profits and there is some suspicion that even these are understated due to write-offs of acquisition costs and related charges. Curiously some of these subsidiaries are located in the Cayman Islands, Guernsey and other "tax havens". One wonders just what role these subsidiaries play and whether their existence reduces federal tax revenues in any way. It is a virtual certainty that deregulation has been good for the banks but less so for taxpayers at large.

THE FINAL PUSH

There are a few small bones that banks have been denied until now and a cynic might be forgiven for suspecting this is largely for cosmetic political purposes. The banks have been denied access to the car leasing business and are still not allowed to sell insurance over the counter although they can own insurance companies. Why they should be allowed to do either heaven only knows. Corporations that have licenses to print money should not be allowed to compete with companies that do not. It is not a level playing field by any stretch of the imagination. But on the basis of the track record to date, some generous government which has been the beneficiary of "benevolence" from the banks will capitulate to their wishes, "in the public interest", because bank competition will "lower costs to the consuming public". You could almost bet your bank balance on it.

At the moment, however, the banks have bigger fish to fry — at least some of them do. The biggest of the banks want the right to merge so they will become even bigger. They claim that they are too small to be major players in the globalized banking arena of the future.

The Bank Act does not permit bank mergers due to the 10% rule which prohibits any one person from owning more than 10% of the shares of any Schedule I bank. This rule, according to Charles Baillie, president of the Toronto-Dominion Bank, was put in place in the 1960s because Chase Manhattan of New York wanted to buy his bank.

The TD does not support the bigger banks push toward mergers. According to Baillie a smaller bank is a better bank. "In today's world you succeed by being smarter, by having a good strategy and executing it well. Size is not a strategy. It's a statistic." Baillie was speaking to the annual meeting of his bank in January, 1997, in an attempt to reassure his employees who suspect that the TD would be the first takeover target in a deregulated market and that their jobs would be in jeopardy.

Curiously, after this chapter was written, but before going to press, Baillie told the Task Force on Financial Services that his bank wouldn't object to the 10% ownership rule being dropped "provided consumer choice, system safety and soundness of economic sovereignty are fully considered."[3] It appears that the big three took Baillie out to the woodshed and talked to him. He was responsible enough, however, to link the switch in policy to a good debate including economic sovereignty which is more than the others are asking for.

A Royal Bank study in 1996 observed that Canadian banks have slipped in their world ranking and none are included in the top 50 largely because Japanese banks have grown rapidly in the last 20 years. But anyone who has studied Japanese banks knows that they have a certain puff-ball quality which has to be taken into account for a proper evaluation. Their assets, which include shares in publicly traded companies, are not as solid as their balance sheets portray.

A more relevant question is how Canadian banks rank in North America. The Royal and CIBC are currently sixth and seventh in total assets, virtually unchanged from sixth and eighth in 1977. That, in my opinion, is big enough. Obviously the big banks don't agree.   They have been waging a propaganda war to convince Canadians that bank mergers are necessary if we are to play in the major league, and that mergers are inevitable in the kind of world in which we live.

It is interesting to note in reading old newspaper clippings that every time the Bank Act comes up for review and the banks call for change "in the public interest" that we are subject to a massive propaganda campaign.   The Canadian Bankers Association launches an all-out lobbying effort. The financial papers are willing allies.

This time the *Financial Post* was lead batter with its editorial of April 12, 1996, "Canadian banks need size to compete internationally."   It said: "Canada's banks are only minnows in the world fish pond. The biggest bank in the world is Japan's newly merged Bank of Tokyo-Mitsubishi Ltd. with assets of $U.S. 86-billion; that's five times bigger than any Canadian bank."[4] This was followed up a few days later in the Dominion Bond Rating Service Ltd's. latest banking industry review lauding banks and saying they face consolidation because there are too many for the size of the Canadian market. The DBRS wisdom was duly reported in both the *Financial Post* and the *Globe and Mail* on April 26, 1996.

In October, 1996, Bank of Montreal Chief Matthew Barrett called on Ottawa to allow mergers among the Big Six so they can meet competition over the next decade. He was honest enough to admit that, "It is inescapable, if there are mergers, there will be some adjustments." Analysts have predicted up to 10,000 jobs could be lost if two of the big banks merge.[5] The Canadian banks may claim that they are not big enough to compete internationally but when it comes to propaganda they are world-class.

On Friday, June 20, 1997, the *Globe and Mail* ran a full page lead editorial entitled "Carve up the sacred cow of bank ownership" in which it opined that the time had come to end the 10% limitation on bank ownership in order to facilitate mergers and the potential takeover by foreigners. It acknowledged, however, that there could be negative consequences for the Canadian economy if the whole industry were foreign controlled.[6]

A few days later the Bank of Montreal released a 69-page document entitled "Policy Alternatives for Canadian Financial Services" as its contribution to the Task Force set up by the Minister of Finance to advise the government on changes required in the financial services industry. Canada's third largest bank is plumping for further deregulation of the financial services industry , an end to the prohibition against car leasing and over the counter insurance sales by the banks and, most significant of all, "the 10% limit on shareholdings by any single interest should be amended to allow for the takeover of domestic banks by widely held foreign institutions."[7]

Wow! At least you have to give the Bank of Montreal high marks for honesty in calling a spade a spade. Already you can sense the high cards being passed back and forth under the table in this high stakes poker game. The Task Force will be delighted because one gets the sense that rather than an independent arbiter of the public interest, it is primarily a handmaiden of the government in coming up with the evidence to support the changes already in the government's plan. The Task Force is part of what we call "due process".

One would have to be blind to consider it impartial. Its first chairman, Bay Street lawyer Jim Baillie, is widely touted for his expertise in financial matters but was that any reason to believe that public hearings were not necessary. And was he not pre-judging the outcome of Task Force deliberations when he told the press that "big" was not necessarily "bad" even before a preliminary report was prepared? Then for him to believe that he could discuss with Hal Jackman the possible sale of National Trust to the Bank of Nova Scotia and just turn the file over to a partner to execute the deal without any notion of conflict of interest was naivety in the extreme.

No senior partner in a big Toronto law firm could be impartial in a matter of this kind. They earn huge fees acting for the banks, so does anyone think they could be party to a report that concluded the banks were big enough or too big already? Two other members of the Task Force are bank directors. Does anyone suggest that they could consider banks' powers with true objectivity? Other members of the Task Force work for or with organizations relying on bank credit. Are they likely to bite the hand that feeds them?

One is driven to the conclusion that the deck is stacked. The report of the Task Force, unless its new chairman is dominant enough to wag the dog, should be taken with a grain of salt. One wonders why the public should pay for it? It would be more appropriate for the banks to pick up the tab. The government could give the savings to critics of the banks in order to hold their own public hearings and learn what ordinary citizens have to say about their banks and financial institutions.

LOOKING INTO THE FUTURE

The bottom line is that the big banks intend to push relentlessly for amalgamation and takeover. They want to help finance the dash toward oligopoly on a world scale. They want to benefit from the big fees involved in mergers, takeovers and leveraged buyouts as well as expand their activity in merchant banking.

But how much of this is good for Canada and Canadians? Not much! If we only had two or three banks, instead of six, competition would be even less and they would be even more difficult to deal with than they are now.

Should Canada sign the Multilateral Agreement on Investment, and there is every reason to believe that we will as our government is one of its promoters, our big banks will be sitting ducks for takeover by American or other foreign banks and there wouldn't be a thing we could do about it short of expropriation.

Maritimers and Westerners in particular are sensitive to injustices created when banking power is centralized. Deposits collected in the East and West are invested in the big cities of Central Canada. The same sense of injustice would be felt by the whole country if decision-making authority was based elsewhere.

The whole trend toward centralization of financial power and its globalization under MAI and similar agreements is the genesis of the Evil Empire of world autocracy. Once we really understand where the train is taking us we may want to get off before it is too late.

CHAPTER 7

AN F GRADE FOR THE MEDIA

"If our nation can issue a dollar bond it can issue a dollar bill. The element that makes bonds good makes bills good also. "

Thomas Edison

The main problem with the press is their profound lack of interest in the functioning of the economic system. Of course they are curious to know whether the economy will grow 2.7%, 3.5% or not at all; whether the Canadian dollar will rise or fall and at what level the Bank of Canada will intervene; and whether the jobless rate will be 9.3% or 8.7% next year. Opinions on all these subjects make news and the media rely heavily on a stable of bank and brokerage house economists without acknowledging that, with one or two noteworthy exceptions, they are little more than propagandists for the financial institutions that employ them. This fact alone results in a strongly biased financial and business press.

The economics I would like the media to discuss is why the Bank of Canada felt it necessary to bring on two horrendous recessions that created mayhem in the Canadian economy? What alternatives were considered and why were they rejected? Why

66

have interest rates in the 1990s been so much higher than traditional levels and who benefits from such a policy? Why has the unemployment rate been so high for so long and should consistently high unemployment be considered a national scandal? How can you balance a budget with so many people unemployed?

CHART 2

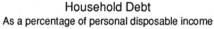

Household Debt
As a percentage of personal disposable income

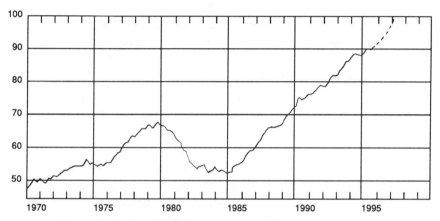

Sources: Bank of Canada Review and Royal Bank

Why do bank economists worry so much about the federal debt when it is the total debt — federal, provincial, municipal, corporate and individual that counts? Reducing the government's debt by downloading it onto the backs of ordinary citizens is no solution. Bankrupting businesses and reducing the taxpayer to an impoverished state, by transferring the debt to them, only makes matters worse. As Chart 2 indicates, personal debt will reach 100% of after tax income by the end of 1997. Finally, why is it that all countries in the world are so far in debt? Is it because they always have been run by profligate politicians? Or does it have something to do with the way money is created? These are the questions the media should be asking but which they persistently sweep under the journalistic rug.

AN ALTERNATIVE TO RECESSION

My first big brush with media indifference on the large questions came in the Spring of 1993. Bank of Canada Governor John Crow appeared determined to wrestle inflation to the ground, even at the expense of breaking almost every bone in the body politic. His tight money policies were extending the recession more or less indefinitely. I knew that there was a far kinder and more effective way of controlling inflation but no one was talking about it.

I thought that if some reputable economist could be convinced, then the press would have to take note. Mike McCracken, president of Informetrica Limited, an Ottawa-based economics firm, was the first name to come to mind. McCracken had written several articles about incomes policies so I knew his mind was not mired in the conventional wisdom. A telephone call was enough to arrange lunch with Mike and his vice-president, Carl Sonnen.

When we met I explained what I would like them to do. I asked if their computer could turn the clock back to 1969 and compare what would have happened if an incomes policy that I had been recommending for about 25 years had been implemented at that time; and the monopoly power of big business and labor curbed as an alternative to the carpet-bombing administered by the Bank of Canada. Informetrica's machine, which was geared to future forecasting, had never attempted a retrospect so they warned that it would be a somewhat lengthy process. With so much at stake I gave the go ahead.

It didn't take long to determine that starting as early as 1969 would be an expensive process — given the need to extend data backwards and to simulate an alternative to the wage and price control program introduced by the Trudeau government in 1975. So we finally settled on the 1978-1985 period which included the devastating 1981-82 recession. It took a few trial runs before the process could be fine-tuned but eventually everyone was satisfied with the authenticity of the results. Carl Sonnen, who was in charge of the project, wrote the report and Mike McCracken reviewed it. The results were fantastic![1]

In the course of the study Sonnen had become convinced that the alternative policy was the right one for Canada, so Informetrica agreed to a joint press conference to release the results. The Ottawa press gallery was booked for Thursday morning, April 8, 1993, and everything was set. Alas, when the morning came, and with only a few minutes notice, we were bumped from our time slot by Prime Minister Brian Mulroney's Chief of Staff, Hugh Segal, who wished to announce to the press that he would not be running to fill his boss' shoes as leader of the Progressive Conservative Party. Then we were bumped again by Liberal spokesmen Herb Gray and Don Boudria who wanted to decry the latest rise in unemployment.

By the time we got started most of the political reporters had scurried off to do their Segal stories and we were left with a handful of stalwarts including several financial writers. As the conference was carried live on the parliamentary press gallery network, and the questioning was extensive, I assumed that the story would be picked up that way or from the press kits which were widely distributed.

The results of the computer simulation showed that the introduction of a simple incomes policy in 1978 would have resulted in 870,000 more jobs in Canada by 1985. Also, interest rates would have been lower, so nearly all those tens of thousands of people who lost their homes, farms and businesses due to high interest rates would have been able to hang on. Debts of governments — federal and provincial — would have been $50-billion to $82-billion less, depending on the assumption about the amount the Canadian dollar would have appreciated versus the U.S. dollar. Sonnen extrapolated the debt figures to 1992 and concluded that the debts of the federal and provincial governments would have been $220-billion less. Finally, inflation would have been only 2.7% in 1985, assuming no appreciation of the Canadian dollar, or 0.5% assuming appreciation, compared to the 4.7% Bank of Canada Governor Gerald Bouey had achieved with his horrendous policy.

I got up early Good Friday morning to see what the press had to say. I could hardly believe the response. There was nothing.   Nothing!   Not one word in any Canadian periodical, radio or TV show that I am aware of. I had spent $30,000 to prove a point with zero results. I would have thought that some serious reporter, somewhere, would have asked the question: "Do you mean to say that with a simple incomes policy we could have avoided the worst effects of the recession, wound up with 870,000 more jobs, $220-billion less debt and much less inflation?" That is exactly what we were saying. The blackout that Friday morning was even more galling because the papers were full of economic trivia.

We had been close to a break when *Macleans* editor Kevin Doyle, whom I had spoken to in advance, agreed to do a feature story with editorial comment. Unfortunately that was the week he was sent on "holidays". In the shuffle of finding his replacement, interest in the story was lost. *Southam* management, proclaiming economic illiteracy, deferred to *Ottawa Citizen* editor Nick Hills, whose understanding of the subject was not noticeably better than that of head office.

Finally, in desperation, I sent a copy of the report with a plaintive letter to *Globe and Mail* columnist, and one of the Ottawa press gallery's brightest lights, Jeffrey Simpson. Unfortunately Simpson was just leaving on sabbatical at the time so he didn't write about it; and from his subsequent columns on economic affairs, it appears that he has not yet grasped the subtleties of the subject. Pity!

MONETARY REFORM

Meanwhile the monetarists' high interest rate policies had let the debt genie out of the bottle. Debt clocks began to appear. Both the nature and magnitude of economic problems began to change rapidly. The simple incomes policy which, had it been implemented prior to the 1981-82 recession, would have allowed the system to muddle along for a few more decades without a major meltdown, was no longer capable of preventing the catastrophe. More heroic measures were required including a complete reversal of the Bank of Canada's decision to get out of the money-creation business.

So, after almost 50 years of keeping "mum" about the fractional reserve system of banking, which has been the principal cause of 45 recessions and depressions in the last 200 years, I decided that silence was no longer morally defensible. I have to shout what I believe to be the truth from the hill tops, whether or not anyone is listening. It is not absolutely inevitable that we have another crash but we will unless we change the system radically. Why will the system crash again? The answer is, if I may mock paraphrase the traditionalists, "because of the fundamentals". You can't have a banking system pumping up credit and debt at an unsustainable rate without having the bubble burst eventually.

Let me repeat one more time. If nearly all the new money which is created each year is created by privately-owned banks, which is true, and if all of that money is created as debt on which interest has to be paid, which is true, and if no one creates any money with which to pay that interest what do you have to do? The answer is, you must borrow more money with which to pay the interest on what you already owe and go deeper and deeper into debt. It is as simple as that.

FUNNY MONEY

So I wrote a book entitled *Funny Money* which includes a little monetary history, a brief description of how the system works and a prescription for changes which would allow it to work consistently well, i.e. without the periodic recessions and depressions we have known. Major changes include the infusion of enough government-created money (GCM) to put a cap on the total debt to GDP ratio, and an incomes policy to prevent the recurrence of the wage-price spiral once full employment and optimum output is achieved.

In the course of my research I asked about 100 of my friends and colleagues if they knew where money came from. The sample included people from all walks of life including doctors, lawyers, brokers, teachers, business people and others — a wide cross-section. Most of them were uncomfortable with the question but when I pushed gently they said that the government printed it. The lowest estimate of GCM was 60% and the highest 100% — which would be a very, very different system than the one we have. Interestingly, not one in the whole hundred had what you could call a working knowledge of the monetary system. So I guess it should have been no surprise to find the same situation with the media.

Diane Francis, *Financial Post* editor, was the first writer I contacted with a view to promoting the book and a good public debate. As we lunched at the Ontario Club it became very clear that her principal interests were overspending and carelessness on the part of government and not macro economics. Efficient government was a common concern but I explained that there were even greater issues to be addressed including the banking system and the debt. When I told her about a new simulation Informetrica had done to track the impact of an infusion of GCM she became quite interested and said she would review the book. She also asked me to write a series of articles, similar to one I had done for the *Financial Post* when John Godfrey was editor, as soon as the book was published.

The next interview was with Peter Cook, a *Globe and Mail* financial columnist. He was very nice to talk to and made no pretence of understanding monetary theory. His reserved personality was a total contrast with the lively and open-minded Diane Francis, and his traditional outlook was steeped in the conventional wisdom. About the only thing the two had in common was that neither knew where money comes from.

The next person on my list was Lloyd Robertson, the almost perennial news anchor for the CTV network and someone for whom I have the utmost respect. We met for lunch at L'Auberge du Pommier, which is Lloyd's favorite north-Toronto eatery. I gave him the usual pitch and he seemed interested despite a limited background in the subject. I got the impression that nothing would happen, however, because he said that in two years he would be turning his anchor position over to someone else and he would then be doing editorials — the implication being that he might be helpful at that time. My response, to paraphrase J.M, Keynes, was that, "In two years we might all be dead."

Lloyd did add some insight into my favorite subject, the banks, in the course of swapping stories. CTV had carried a report by *Globe and Mail* columnist Douglas Goold to the effect that the Royal Bank wouldn't be able to juggle its books to keep its profits (1994) below $1-billion as it had on one previous occasion. Well, the Royal demanded an apology and it took days to calm Alan Taylor, the bank's bombastic chairman, while the CTV newsroom held firm against the pressure. Lloyd thought the bank was exercising "raw power". That is the kind of power you can exercise if you have a license to print money.

John Bulloch, then president of the Canadian Federation of Independent Business, was not in the media but he had the same kind of power to influence people and generate debate so I wrote him a letter soliciting his support. Typically he replied by sending me some of the Federation propaganda to read and in his letter he said: "Paul, you remind me of our Federation motto, 'We never give up and we never go away.'"

John Honderich, now publisher of the *Toronto Star*, was next on my list. He listened quite intently and said the *Star* would do something. It wasn't long before reporter Jade Hemeon did a feature article which was all positive except for a couple of comments from Bay Streeters who obviously had not read the book. There was no change in the *Star's* editorial policy, however. It insisted that Finance Minister Paul Martin had no alternative but to concentrate on deficit reduction. It also lamented the fact that he was not paying due heed to job creation without explaining precisely how he might pursue both objectives simultaneously.

After Honderich, I met with Paul Godfrey, publisher of the *Toronto Sun*. We met in his office where he listened intently for 40 minutes. According to my diary he told me that I was "a fascinating fellow which he had always known but even more so after listening to me today."[2] Instead of doing something in the *Sun*, however, he suggested that the *Financial Post* would be a better vehicle due to its prestige. He would check with the publisher and report back the following day, which he did.

A few days later friends phoned joyfully to report Diane Francis' absolutely splendid review of the incomes policy outlined in *Funny Money*. There wasn't a negative word in the whole column. Nor was there a single word about monetary policy — just as if the subject had never been mentioned. Meanwhile I had sent the *Financial Post* the series of four articles that Diane had requested. It was never published. The final article said that globalization was the road to world hegemony and obviously that idea was too avant garde for someone at the paper.

Some months later, following a private discussion, *Toronto Sun* editor John Downing wrote an extremely good review of *Funny Money*.[3] It was a publicists' dream and far more flattering than one would write oneself. Regrettably, however, it had zero impact on *Sun* editorial policy.

A day after my visit to the *Sun* I went to the *Globe and Mail* for afternoon tea with Wm. Thorsell, Editor-in-Chief. He listened carefully and concluded the interview by saying that he would read the book and then discuss it with some of his colleagues. I suspected immediately that it was a lost cause because his colleagues at that time would have included Andrew Coyne, whose feet are so firmly embedded in the concrete of 19th-century laissez-faire economics that the world's most powerful bulldozer couldn't pull him out.

On the theory that one should never give up, I sent copies of my book to a number of journalists beginning with Peter Newman who had been writing some reasonably interesting articles about the economy. No response. Dalton Camp seemed to be a logical ally. He has become far more compassionate since he got a new heart and my wife says he often sounds more like me than me — which I doubted he would view as a compliment, despite the suspicion that he must have been given a liberal heart.

Peter Gzowski seemed like a natural. His program was widely respected and he had orthodox economists on so often that it seemed only fair that a little air time be provided for a contrary opinion. When that idea failed I tried the irrepressible Rex Murphy. Surely, I thought, this is the kind of controversial subject that should excite him. Apparently it didn't.

The quest for media support and interest continued for almost two years — through 1995 and most of 1996 — but with a dismal lack of success. Occasionally a radio host would say a few kind words and the Montréal papers wrote balanced stories but the total impact on the public consciousness was minimal despite the fact that people who read *Funny Money* and its sequel, *Surviving the Global Financial Crisis: The Economics of Hope for Generation X*, were in most cases favorably impressed. I regret to say that with the lack of media attention (no Canadian paper reviewed *Surviving the Global Financial Crisis*) the impact was invisible. The only remaining hope was to try to make monetary reform a central issue in a federal election campaign in the belief that the press would have to address the issue seriously. It was a vain hope.

THE CANADIAN ACTION PARTY (CAP)

The Canadian Action Party is a coalition of concerned Canadians. Its original membership comprised people who voted eight different ways in the 1993 election, but its efforts to introduce fresh thinking in the political realm were seriously undermined when Prime Minister Jean Chrétien called an early election which left us scrambling to field candidates and only two weeks to campaign. In addition our platform was given scant attention by the press. Worse, most of what was reported was cynical in the extreme.

A number of reports, including a CTV commentary, referred to CAP as "the party that wants to print money". It wasn't the bald fact that was objectionable but the sneering innuendo that there is some kind of money which is not printed — excluding coins which are minted. Apart from coins all money is printed — some on fine paper by the Bank of Canada (legal tender), and the rest by charted banks on computer paper (deposit money or credit money). What made the reports most objectionable is that the sneers came from the lips of reporters who didn't have a clue about what money is or where it comes from.

Most reporters accept the notion that the economists can't all be wrong. This is a naive assumption for skeptical journalists especially in the face of a record of performance which includes disastrous recessions, massive unemployment, monumental debt and little hope.

There are some very good economists. There are even some who understand the perils of a fractional reserve or zero reserve banking system. But they are the exceptions. The vast majority are wedded to classroom abstractions that never have made any sense in the real world. Take a look at the record.

Two hundred years after the industrial revolution made it possible to mass produce goods on a scale previously unknown, economists still haven't designed a system for its equitable distribution. During this 200 year period output was far below its potential because economists believed Jean Baptiste Say's law that, "all production creates an equal and opposite demand", so consequently there could be no such thing as a periodic shortage of purchasing power. They were wrong.

At the same time, economists have condoned and rationalized the fractional reserve banking system which has been primarily responsible for 45 recessions and depressions in 200 years. Now they insist that we pay down the debt resulting from that system knowing full well that there isn't enough legal tender in existence. (Canada's federal debt is about $600-billion, our total debt is about $1.8-trillion, yet there is only about $30-billion real, legal tender money in total.)

The mainline economists have told us for almost 20 years that a little short-term pain would lead to long-term gain. Are we entitled to ask them what the gain has been other than massive debt and massive unemployment? They are then brazen enough to rationalize the immoral level of unemployment by calling it "natural".

Traditionalists also insist that all inflation is caused by too much money chasing too few goods. If that were true, why would central bankers like Canada's Gordon Thiessen be so concerned about inflation when Canada and the Western world have vast quantities of goods and services just waiting for someone to buy them. The fact is that store shelves are loaded to the brim and bankruptcies are occurring daily because there are too few customers with disposable cash.

The list could go on but the point is that expert opinion, too, is open to challenge and this is especially true of economics which undoubtedly has the worst track record of all professions. Here is an acid test for journalists to apply. The next time you interview an economist, ask to see his or her plan to cap and/or reduce the total debt to GDP ratio — not federal debt, but the total federal, provincial, municipal, corporate and personal debt. If they are able to produce such a plan the discovery will be as rare as finding a diamond in a gravel pit.

There was at least one exception to the media rule. In "Personally Speaking", Victoria *Times Colonist* editorialist, Paul Minvielle, wrote a column entitled: "Listen hard to Hellyer's message."[4] He admitted that he might not have been receptive had he not read part of *Funny Money: A Common Sense Alternative to Mainline Economics*. But after having done so, he said: "The fact is, I've become convinced the Bank of Canada has abrogated its fiscal responsibilities, and that the Canadian economy and the creation of money shouldn't be left to the commercial banks."[5] One paper in all of Canada, but at least it's a start.

Unless the media becomes interested in these issues, in a major and relentless way, there is no hope of Canada ending the millennium with a bang or of avoiding another crash. What could be more of a challenge for genuine investigative journalism?

CHAPTER 8

GLOBALIZATION:
THE EVIL EMPIRE

"The Canadians don't know what they have signed.
In twenty years they will be sucked into the U.S. economy. "

Clayton Yeutter[1]

There are profound rumblings in the global marketplace. Trade barriers are being dismantled as never before. But all the talk about world trade is primarily a camouflage for the real blueprint which is all about investment, ownership and control. We are witnessing a bloodless coup d'état by the world financial system. The result, if unchecked, will be a world autocracy of central banks, international banks and the giant global corporations they control.

Regrettably, most of the people I talk to are quite unaware of what is going on. The concept of globalization has been sold so subtly that it is now accepted as "inevitable", if not a *fait accompli*. They have no knowledge of the extent to which nation states are losing their sovereignty and the potential impact on their own lives and fortunes.

Former world leaders are more in tune with the times and recognize the imminent peril. A group of former presidents and prime ministers who met in Vancouver in May, 1996, under the chairmanship of Canada's Pierre Trudeau, issued a strong warning that globalization threatens to overwhelm societies unless today's political leaders respond more effectively.

An issue of "deepest concern" they said in a communique, "is the inability to date of governments, international institutions and private sector actors to design their economic policies and activities to overcome the current high levels of unemployment, social disparity and political instability so evident in countries both industrialized and developing."[2]

Moreover, "a most disturbing consequence of present trends toward globalization and privatization are the increasing disparities in income and economic well-being among countries and within countries. These must be contained."[3]

The former world leaders, with their wider perspective based on vast experience, have good reasons to be concerned and it is a matter of deep regret that we have given little, if any, heed to their warning and continue to rocket blindly ahead as if a new golden age were just over the horizon.

THE MULTILATERAL AGREEMENT ON INVESTMENT

Early in the Spring of 1997 some Vancouver members of the newly formed Canadian Action Party (CAP) sent me some material about the Multilateral Agreement on Investment. At first incredulous, the more I read the greater became my concern. Candidates were advised to raise the subject as an election issue, which they did, and the New Democratic Party subsequently joined the chorus. Liberal candidates pleaded ignorance. Even though the treaty had been under negotiation for two years, the government had seen no necessity of advising its own supporters what it had in mind for Canada.

By the time our election brochure was written, CAP members felt so strongly about the issue that the item shouted "MAI-DAY" and warned that if the Liberals were re-elected it was "Goodbye Canada". The wording sounded a bit extreme at the time but, in retrospect, I think it was dead on.

As voters began to show some interest, Liberal candidates were given a fixed statement to read. Trade Minister Art Eggleton felt obliged to tell CBC Radio listeners that the MAI was a wonderful deal for Canada. It would encourage foreign investment and create jobs. It would help Canadian companies investing abroad, and Canada's national interests would be fully protected. Half-way through the polemic, the image in my mind was of the serpent in the garden of Eden saying, "Go ahead, take my word it will be good for you." Eggleton's words were so smooth that I knew they would convince most voters who were not well versed in the opposite view.

• • •

The MAI is, in reality, a bill of rights for international banks and global corporations. Someone dubbed it "NAFTA on steroids". Its purpose is to provide risk-free and problem-free investment opportunities for international corporations — benefits gained at the expense of national sovereignty and national advantage.

We are told that the idea originated with the U.S. Council for International Business, an organization whose members will be principal beneficiaries. The concept is consistent with the dogma of unregulated capitalism and is strongly supported by the world's most powerful industrial nations. Why Canada is one of the leading champions of the new treaty is a total mystery unless we want to play the role of water-boy to the U.S. Canada has little, if anything, to gain and virtually everything to lose.

The MAI grants to citizens and corporations of all 29-member countries of the OECD "citizen status" in host countries. Consequently, they can never be discriminated against by any government at any level, on any account, such as their contribution to the welfare of citizens of the host country. Serving the interests of the host country is deemed to be "protectionist" and consequently prohibited. (The hypocrisy of this measure is the strong support of the major industrial powers which became major industrial powers as a result of "protectionist" measures.)

• • •

Accordingly, the MAI has written into its detailed draft articles the rights of transnational corporations:

- to export their commodities or services across all borders to other societies' markets with no conditions attached;
- to unilaterally purchase and own any structure or productive capacity of any other signatory nation with no requirement to sustain its viability, employment level or location in the home country;
- to own any saleable natural resource of other countries and to have national right to any concession, licence or authorization to extract its oil, forest, mineral or other resources with no obligation to sustain these resources, or to use them in the interest of the host society;
- to bid for and own any privatized public infrastructure, social good or cultural transmission without any limit of foreign control permitted by law;
- to have access to any domestic government grant, loan, tax incentive or subsidy with the same rights as any domestic firm, with no means test, locale requirement, or public-interest distinction permitted;
- to be free of any and all performance requirements of job creation, domestic purchase of goods, import/export reciprocation, and technology or knowledge transfer to the host society;
- to repel as illegal any national standards of human rights, labor rights or environmental protection on goods produced in and imported from other regions or nations.[4]

"We will oppose," stated the President of the U.S. Council for International Business in a letter to U.S. officials on March 21, 1997, "any and all measures to create or even imply binding obligations for governments or business related to environment and labor."[5]

This is one of the most significant features of unregulated capitalism. Corporations are undoing 100 years of social progress by moving their operations from countries that forbid child labor and enforce environmental protection laws, to countries that don't. And the MAI is designed to protect their rights to exploit children, maintain sweatshops and commit environmental atrocities without fear that their goods can be barred entry into any country for those reasons.

WHAT THE MAI MEANS TO CANADA

In a word, it would mean that we could no longer legislate in our own best interests. We would no longer be able to attach conditions to foreign investment such as where to locate, how many Canadians to hire, whether or not some research should be done in Canada and whether there would be a sharing of "know-how". We could not insist that our resources be processed and have value added in Canada.

Our upstart industries would be vulnerable. If they succeeded in gaining an increased share of a market dominated by foreign companies they could be bought and shut down by a foreign company. There would be no requirement to sell the machinery to Canadian workers who would be out of luck. At the same time the foreign raider would be guaranteed unrestricted access for its products.

A variation on this theme occurred after the Free Trade Agreement (FTA) was signed. For years, Rubberset Co. had been the principal employer in the small town of Gravenhurst, Ontario. With the border removed it "rationalized" its operation by closing the Gravenhurst plant and moving production to the United States. A plea from the workers to buy the plant and machinery fell on deaf ears.

We would be unable to amend or improve environmental laws for fear of being sued by foreign corporations as we have already learned from the FTA. Canadian legislators' hands would be tied when considering a whole range of laws for a safer, saner Canada.

We would be unable to protect our cultural industries. The Americans covet unrestricted access for culture industries and are determined to get it by hook or by crook. They were upset that we got an exemption under the FTA and the North

American Free Trade Agreement (NAFTA). They cracked the wall when the World Trade Organization ruled against Canada's attempt to stop *Sports Illustrated* magazine from printing a Canadian edition stuffed with U.S. content. Now they are determined to use MAI to capture the rest of the prize.

When he was trade minister, Art Eggleton talked of getting an exemption for existing Canadian cultural policies, but as the MAI treaty proponents plan, such an exemption would be quite limited — a will o' the wisp. "The agreement will be based on a stand-still agreement and a rollback principle," according to Marinus Sikkel, a Dutch official. Under the stand-still provision, Canada would be prevented from introducing any new measures to deal with culture, including any response to the challenges of new technologies. Rollback means abandoning existing policies for the protection of cultural industries over time.

What this means is the ultimate elimination of barriers to takeovers of all kinds. Nothing would be exempt, including books and magazines. There would be no Canadian content requirements for TV and radio, and no special tax deductions for Canadian advertisers patronizing Canadian TV, radio and magazines. We would lose any remaining provisions to ensure that Canadian voices are heard. Media giants from south of the border would be able to remove all remaining roadblocks to complete domination of the Canadian cultural scene.[6]

MAI IS A TRAVESTY OF CAPITALISM

I was always taught that one of the tenets of capitalism was that investors took risks in the hope of gaining substantial rewards. It seemed like a fair game — a bit of a gamble but one where careful planning, good thinking and a modicum of luck would produce more winners than losers.

The MAI is the dream-child of a different breed of capitalist. These are managers who have made the big time in the corporate world, have received handsome rewards and who now want to keep getting richer and richer in a risk-free world ripe for exploitation. The concept is a travesty of capitalism.

WHO NEEDS MAI?

No one!   One of the excuses Art Eggleton gave for Canada's support for MAI is that more foreign investment would follow and consequently more jobs.   Of course he provided no proof that this would be the case nor that it would be good for Canada.   Neither did he say that it has been Canadian-owned business which has created the new jobs in recent years whereas foreign-owned business has reduced its total number of employees in Canada.

Nothing in recent years has been more saddening than the spectacle of Prime Minister Chrétien and senior ministers beating the foreign bushes for increased investment in Canada instead of staying at home and spanking the banks to make them provide adequate credit to Canadian entrepreneurs.   Canada already has one of the highest levels of foreign ownership in the industrialized world, second only to Australia, and the costs are enormous.   They will be even greater in the years ahead. Furthermore, according to a United Nations report called the World Investment Report, about two-thirds of mergers and acquisitions in Canada for the 1991-1993 period involved foreign investors.[7]   The immediate result of this activity is more downsizing with a loss of jobs.   The long-term result is a greater outflow of profits, interest, dividends and royalties — a drain on our foreign exchange reserves that we can ill afford.

One alleged benefit to Canada, according to Eggleton's list, is easier access to foreign markets for Canadian corporations.   In trying to think which companies might benefit one comes up with a very short list, including the banks.   They are already doing quite well in foreign markets, according to their annual reports, and that seems to be where they are concentrating their attention rather than on a prosperous Canada.   If all impediments are removed they will get even fatter.   That will make them even more attractive targets for foreign takeovers.   Then, as what remains of our economic independence is lost, so, too, will be the determination of our destiny.

FTA AND NAFTA REVISITED

When the Free Trade Agreement was negotiated in 1987 it was sold to Canadians, to the extent that we bought it, as a trade agreement. What we were getting, we were told, was guaranteed access to U.S. markets.

That promise was a mirage. We never have had, and never will have, guaranteed access to the U.S. market. Just ask the people who have been selling steel, cement, softwood lumber, wheat, mens suits and other products. The Americans still throw up barriers of one kind or another when their markets are subject to intense competition.

In reality the FTA was only superficially about trade. It was primarily about investment. The Americans wanted guaranteed access to our resources and our industries — all of our industries. We held out on a couple of fronts, including cultural industries, but these hold-outs have never been accepted and are now being revisited in the MAI negotiations because the Americans want the same access to Canada that they have to California.

With the FTA, President Ronald Reagan accomplished with one stroke of the pen what American armies had been unable to do in 1776 and 1812. He conquered Canada. Brian Mulroney ran up the white flag. Of course it may take twenty years, or less, to substitute the stars and stripes for the maple leaf but that will depend on the rate of foreign investment in Canada — a rate that will be beyond our control.

Limits to Canadian independence have already appeared as a result of the FTA. In 1990 the Ontario New Democratic Party promised to introduce provincial auto insurance as Saskatchewan, Manitoba and British Columbia had done. Personally, I am not a fan of provincially-run auto insurance schemes but I believe that a government elected on that platform should be able to implement it. State Farm, the U.S. insurance giant, threatened to sue Ontario under the FTA for $1.3-billion in loss of profits, and potential profits, if it went ahead. The Ontario government abandoned the plan.

More recently the federal government banned the fuel

additive MMT from gasoline. The U.S. giant Ethyl Corporation is suing Ottawa for $192-million under the FTA even
though MMT is not permitted in the United States.

These cases are but the tip of the iceberg concerning
suits that might arise due to changes in environmental laws or
the introduction of new social legislation such as universal
dental or drug plans or, in fact, any federal, provincial,
municipal or First Nations program of any kind that threatens
the control or profit of American corporations in Canada. MAI
would extend the same suffocating rights to corporations of 27
additional countries.

I am not the least bit convinced that Canada can survive
unless the FTA and NAFTA are abrogated. There might be
a hypothetical case that we could hang on for a while by the
skin of our teeth if the Canadian banks all remain Canadian and
become fiercely nationalistic in their lending and investment
policies. But it is stretching credibility to think that our bankers
could have such a change of heart. Mr. Justice Lloyd Houlden,
who heard the T. Eaton Company bankruptcy protection
application, said he almost had to get down on his knees to
persuade the Bank of Nova Scotia not to bounce Eaton's
cheques. The fact that a great Canadian institution was at stake
didn't appear to matter.

THE CONNECTION BETWEEN GLOBALIZATION AND BANKING

You may wonder why a book that is primarily
concerned about the evil consequences of unrestricted global
investment is equally concerned about money and banking. It
is because the two are inextricably linked. With the existing
fractional reserve or zero reserve banking system whoever can
create the most credit money will rule the world. Banks manufacture money to lend to corporations to buy other peoples
assets — mines, forests and factories. In fact Canadian banks
have assisted large foreign corporations by lending them credit
money with which to buy real Canadian assets.

On a world scale it is obvious that no small country like

Canada is in the same league as the United States, Japan or Germany. Even if our banks were allowed to merge, their amalgamated conglomerates could buy us out overnight and probably covet the opportunity to do so. For this reason our government must not tamper with the 10% limitation on ownership of Canadian banks. To do so would be to invite disaster in our financial services industry. We are in enough peril already without losing our banks which, in theory at least, could provide the last bulwark against extinction.

GOODBYE CANADA?

It should be clear to anyone with the ability to project a few years ahead, that the future of our country hangs by a thread. That is already true under the FTA and NAFTA. To sign MAI would be the final nail in our coffin.

The reason for such a dire prediction can be found in the abrogation period. Under the FTA and NAFTA the conquest of Canada is only tentative. If the pressure gets too great we can do the "Houdini act" and escape in 6 months. Under MAI the abrogation period would be 5 years, with 15 years extended protection for foreign corporations already established. Once the MAI is signed, the conquest would be permanent.

You can see now why the MAI has been negotiated in secret and why none of its principal promoters wanted it raised in recent election campaigns in Canada, France and Britain. The Chrétien government went to extraordinary lengths to stifle discussion which only underlines the seriousness of the issue.

So where are the nationalists when we need them? Sure the *Toronto Star* carried a lead editorial on May 28, 1997 entitled "Swept Under the Rug" which outlined clearly the disadvantages of MAI to Canada. But there was a time when it would have shouted, "Stop the MAI," in 120-point type on its front page. Where are the Keith Davey's, Jim Coutts and Eddie Goodman's of old? Will they just doze on until they are wakened from their reverie by the sounding of the Last Post? And where is the political party that will fight for Canada?

CHAPTER 9

TOO MANY POLITICAL PARTIES

*"Politics is perhaps the only profession for which
no preparation is thought necessary. "*

Yosida-Torajiro

It is my firmly held conviction that there are too many political parties in Canada. Then why on earth, you might ask, would I help form a new one at this stage of my life? The answer, to put it bluntly, is too many parties but too little real choice.   Three basically conservative parties, one labor dominated party and one separatist party offer little choice to middle-of-the-road liberals and progressives. I looked at the programs of all the major parties and concluded that I could not, in conscience, vote for any one of them. Many of my friends felt exactly the same way though I suspect that most of them, on June 2, 1997, held their noses and voted for the major party that they perceived to be the least of evils.

I say "perceived" because there was so little serious debate of the real issues that it was difficult to know what any of the parties would actually do, if elected. The connection between the monetary system and economic performance, for example, was not discussed at all. And the Multilateral Agreement on Investment, which has to be one of the most important issues facing Canada since 1867, was studiously avoided except for a couple of brief references by NDP leader Alexa McDonough in the dying days of the campaign. The distribution of income was not an issue. The same was true of the pension system which is in total disarray. National unity only became an issue toward the end of the campaign and then in a predominately superficial and unhelpful way.

The media noted the superficiality of the debate — especially after the election when it was too late for them to do anything about it. While the campaign was actually on they were more like a school of trained fish rising to the bait of managed news and photo opportunities. To be totally fair, however, it is not easy to force political leaders and parties to debate important issues if they stubbornly refuse to.

THE LIBERAL PARTY

The Chrétien Liberals have been the disappointment of my life. They have abandoned too many Liberal principles and broken too many promises to be worthy of the name. They promised to eliminate the GST and didn't. They could have kept the promise if they had really wanted to because there are at least two areas of taxation that would have produced an equivalent revenue while eliminating the bureaucratic nightmare and vast underground economy associated with the GST. One is a financial transaction tax along the lines proposed by Jack Biddell in his book, *A Self-Reliant Future for Canada*. Or they could have imposed a small turnover tax on all business which would have raised a comparable amount. What was lacking was the will to keep their promise.

The promise to renegotiate the FTA also went by the boards. Worse, the Liberals became a willing accomplice of the Americans in negotiating NAFTA without first eliminating any of the objectionable features of the FTA. Chrétien assumed Mulroney's mantle of continentalism without a murmur of complaint. Pro-Canadian Liberals should be aghast!

Most offensive to me was the Chrétien government's blanket adoption of the Newt Gingrich brand of U.S. neo-conservatism which had been brought to Canada and popularized by Preston Manning and the Reform Party. This was a complete rejection of everything Liberals had stood for from Mackenzie King to Pierre Trudeau. Money's rights ascended over people's rights.

Chrétien and Paul Martin refused to consider genuinely liberal alternatives. I pleaded with them to learn the lesson of history and use the Bank of Canada creatively to provide fiscal flexibility as previous Liberal administrations had done. With help from the Bank of Canada we could have pursued the full employment, high-growth path to a balanced federal budget. Lives would have been saved and hope restored while the deficit would have been reduced just as quickly.

Instead, Chrétien and Martin listened to the high priests of monetarism and laissez-faire economics — a brand of conservatism. Witness the fact that the *Globe and Mail*, in its lead editorial of October 28, 1996, said the Liberal Party was the best party in Canada because it was the most conservative. So this is the standard against which it must be judged. If you were convinced that the deficit was Canada's biggest problem then you give the Chrétien government full marks for attacking it so vigorously. Paul Martin would deserve credit as the driving force behind the policy.

But if you believe, as I believe, that the deficit was not the principal problem, but rather a symptom of much deeper problems including the economic philosophy responsible for the deficit and debt, then you might conclude, as I have concluded, that the Chrétien government has done more damage to Canada than any Liberal government of modern times and that Paul Martin has been the worst finance minister in memory.

PROGRESSIVE CONSERVATIVE PARTY

In retrospect the PC Party really deserved what happened to it in 1993. Too much party first and people last — especially when patronage had been one of the big levers which Brian Mulroney had used to topple John Turner's government. A greater disappointment, though it appeared to play a very small role in the PC defeat, was the FTA, the full consequences of which are not yet fully appreciated.

It was a deep pit from which the new leader, Jean Charest, had to pull an old, tired and balking political horse. With a combination of wit, charm, persistence and hard work he succeeded brilliantly in getting the show back on the road. He had the team, the financing — everything required for success, except a monopoly on conservatism. Why, in this circumstance, he would try to ape the Reform Party and out-Tory the Liberals I do not know. It was either bad advice or bad judgment or some combination of the two.

In fact the Tory platform for the 1997 election was not credible. You cannot cut taxes by $12-billion and make up the difference by further cuts in expenditure, especially when the Liberals had already cut the fat and some of the guts from the federal establishment. There was little of significance left to cut and interfering with many of the remaining items would bring howls of protest as Charest found when most of his caucus came from the Maritime provinces and election promises had to be abandoned.

Even if the plan had been viable, it was not an honest job-creation proposal. Creating jobs in the private sector with the money saved by firing public servants does not result in a net increase in employment. It simply brings a shift in employment from one sector to the other. If that is the aim of the game it is, or was before cuts in government-provided services began to hurt, a legitimate policy. But it shouldn't be sold as job creation which, of course, depends on the amount of money spent rather than on who spends it.

THE REFORM PARTY

It was inevitable, when Canada has been so badly governed for most of the last quarter-century, that a populist party would arise like a phoenix from the western plains. It happened in the 1930s when both the Cooperative Commonwealth Federation, later the NDP, and Social Credit Parties were born. They represented two very different approaches to the same general circumstance — unacceptably bad performance on the part of the central government. The worse it gets the greater the alienation.

What Westerners do not understand is that their frustration is not unique. They assume it is so because of a "we versus them" relationship with the principal villains being Ontario and Québec with their predominant electoral power. It is futile to try to convince Westerners that the dissatisfaction is vertical as well as horizontal although the number of Ontarians who voted Reform in the last two federal elections should give them some hint.

Two issues are symbolic rather than basic — gun control and Québec. Westerners might be surprised to know that people in rural and northern Ontario and Québec share their attitude on gun control as it specifically relates to the registration of rifles and shotguns.

Western attitudes concerning Québec are similar in some respects and different in others. They are similar in the sense that they feel Québec is often pampered and catered to, and a case can be made to support the allegation. Any party in power or party about to assume power will bend a little in the face of such a large block of votes. It's what Pierre Trudeau used to call "power politics". Without being unfair, one suspects that Preston Manning's change in attitude toward Stornaway and other such matters suggest that given a choice between forming a national government or not forming a government, Reform might be willing to bend a bit in Québec's favor.

THE NEW DEMOCRATIC PARTY

Of the major parties, the NDP's 1997 election platform was closest to my heart due to its emphasis on people's needs as opposed to the priority of numbers. It proposed spending more money on health care, education and environmental concerns. The weakness in this approach is that it didn't have a clue where the money would come from. Getting it by taxing the rich, and from higher corporation taxes, were little more than wishful thinking. When people sense they are overtaxed, those that are able to move their money offshore do so. And when industry is overtaxed it moves to greener pastures.

The NDP platform, then, despite its emotional appeal, contained the same fundamental weakness as the platform of the other major parties. It wasn't credible. If they had stood four square for monetary reform, so that you knew the extra money would be coming from the Bank of Canada, it would have been different. There are some monetary reformers in the party, but their views did not prevail and the NDP's nod in the direction of monetary reform was picayune.

There are many important reasons why someone like me, who has been in business all my life, could not support the NDP. Its principal thrust is still anti-business. This is a short-sighted and self-defeating philosophy. For any country to prosper and provide useful jobs and exciting opportunity for its citizens there has to be cooperation between business, government and labor.

The NDP's achilles heel is labor domination. This is an anachronism as we end the twentieth-century. Labor leaders are not willing to accept the idea of an incomes policy that would tie wage increases to the average increase in productivity which is absolutely essential if the economy is to operate at its optimum capacity on a consistent basis. It is, after all, a form of income sharing.

In a chat with the Canadian Labour Congress' Chief Economist, Andrew Jackson, in the Fall of 1996, he admitted the necessity of some form of incomes policy. When it comes to the nitty-gritty, however, most union leaders balk. They can't have it both ways! They can't ask the state to provide all the services they ask for and still expect the economy to operate with a ball and chain on one leg.

BLOC QUEBECOIS

I only include this party because it has elected a large block of MPs, was the official opposition and remains a force in Canadian and especially Québec politics. It is primarily a single issue party dedicated to the breakup of the Canadian federation so its success, or otherwise, is profoundly significant to federalists and separatists alike. It is not a model, however, that one would wish to see emulated in other parts of Canada.

On the political spectrum the Bloc has often shown greater concern for people issues than the three conservative parties. Its membership includes a number of social democrats and social liberals but many of its MPs are nationalists who would leave politics if the federalist side won. For that reason one cannot easily foresee what influence it might bring to bear in the event sovereignty ceased to be an issue.

THE IDEAL

The ideal number of major parties is a subjective judgment. For the sake of argument I am suggesting three. One of these should lean in the direction of minimum government and maximum personal responsibility. Another should lean in the direction of more proactive goals for government and a more extensive social safety net. The third should occupy the middle position half-way between the other two — the position the Liberal Party traditionally held, when it was really liberal, half-way between the Conservative and the NDP. That would give electors a wide range of choice including the option of moving in one direction or the other if the pendulum needed resetting.

One or more of the parties would have to support monetary reform and ensure that the money-creation function was exercised, at least in part, by the people's bank rather than remain the exclusive preserve of private banks. Presumably the same party would impose an incomes policy so the economy could increase its output by that extra 1% necessary to share the wealth more equitably both at home and with the citizens of the world still struggling to acquire the basics we take for granted.

At least one, and preferably all, of the parties should be powerfully pro-Canadian and determined to keep the country intact. Both Reform leader Preston Manning and Québec Premier Lucien Bouchard should re-think their positions and face the reality that if Québec separates it will be the beginning of the end for both distinct societies — Québec and Canada. British Columbia Premier Glen Clark has stated that Canada is unlikely to survive without Québec and I agree totally. The Rest-of-Canada (ROC) wouldn't last twenty years without Québec — my friends say ten — and without Canada it wouldn't be too long before Québec was little more than a Louisiana north. The last significant pocket of French culture in North America would be gone forever.

The breakup of Canada and its piecemeal absorption by the United States would be a tragedy of worldwide dimension. We can and often do play a role that only a close neighbor and friend of the United States can play. We can also point out their shortcomings and suggest that they are leading the world in the wrong direction without fear of their tanks rumbling across our undefended border. Right now we must resist with all our might the U.S. determination to saddle the world with its model through the MAI. If we fail, the question of national unity will be overtaken by the issue of Canadian survival. These are gargantuan questions for all parties to digest.

Just how the re-alignment can be achieved I would hesitate to say. Ideally the Liberal Party should split, with the conservative Liberals going one way and the liberal Liberals another. Either the PC or Reform Party should disappear with the progressives in the PC Party joining with the liberal Liberals. The NDP might continue as the left party with some of its less doctrinaire members joining forces with the liberals and progressives. The Bloc should disappear completely as its *raison d'être* fades with the majority supporting the centre or left-centre parties.

Re-shuffling the political pack should be a good exercise in the months ahead as we try to face some of the important issues that were not addressed in the June 1997 campaign. In deciding where each of us should fit in the politics of tomorrow it is important to begin with a choice of vision.

CHAPTER 10

THE 21st CENTURY

"The world is not, in fact, ruled by global corporations. It is ruled by the global financial system. "

David Korten[1]

As we approach the end of the 20th-century we face some of the most important choices in recorded history. What kind of world do we want? Are we prepared to accept a "new world order" run by big banks and big corporations for the benefit of the wealthy and powerful? A world where nation states count for little and individual voters are powerless? Or do we prefer to keep our national identity and the power to run our own affairs for the benefit of all citizens, rich and poor? A vision of what we want must take shape before we decide which route to follow.

"Let the market decide" is the answer we hear from big business and mainline economists. "Let the invisible hand guide our destiny for the benefit of all." It just happens to be the system which is most beneficial to the richest people on earth and least advantageous to the poor and powerless. Let the lions loose and you can stop worrying about the sheep eating too much grass.

96

The market system is one which accepts that bigger is better. But is it? And how big is too big. At the end of the nineteenth-century when the Rockefellers, Carnegies and Mellons were gobbling up everything in sight, aided and abetted by banking interests who made their own bundle in the process, a public consensus developed that said "Enough is enough". Anti-trust laws were put in place to arrest the process.

With monetarism and the rebirth of laissez-faire capitalism the whole cycle has begun again. But this time the aim of the game is not just U.S. hegemony but world hegemony. Serious competition will be undermined or bought out and new entrants into the market pulverized by their inaccessibility to capital. It is a frightening scenario.

Equally frightening is the attempt to impose a common ideology on the world. When it comes to international cooperation, including financial support, it's the market way or no way. This point was underscored in February, 1996, when the U.S. Senate refused to ratify the nomination of Felix G. Rohatyn to be vice-chairman of the Federal Reserve because Republican Senators considered his views too far outside what they believed to be the economic mainstream.[2] But what if the Senators were wrong, dead wrong, as some of us fervently believe? Any challenge to mainstream thinking was precluded by preventing a debate.

This is the parallel with communism and fascism that Hungarian-born financier George Soros finds so disturbing. Each claimed to be the possessor of ultimate truth but since ultimate truth is not given to humans, these ideologies used oppressive means to impose their views on society. When unfettered capitalism copies this tactic it undermines the very foundation of open and democratic societies.

When one observes how far the playing field has been tilted for the benefit of the rich it is not surprising that a few observers are questioning the efficacy and the morality of laissez-faire capitalism. In his new book, *Everything for Sale: The Virtues and Limits of Markets*, Robert Kuttner argues in favor of rule-bound markets.[3] "There is no other way," he says, "if economic and social chaos is to be avoided."

Governments have provided both the infrastructure for the market and much of the research and development in key areas of economic growth. The benefits of government initiatives have now been privatized while the costs remain in the public domain. It's the whole public and not just shareholders of big corporations who have to maintain the crumbling infrastructure and pay the interest on the debt.

George Soros has been actively promoting western-style organization in Eastern Europe. His experience led him to re-evaluate the American philosophy. He found that "cowboy capitalism" in the former Soviet Union precludes an open society. Excessive individualism causing — "intolerable inequities and instability" — heralds what Soros calls the "capitalist threat" to an open society both in Eastern Europe and the West.[4]

The gains are too unevenly divided. American capitalists have been buying Russian assets at firesale prices while millions of citizens have not been paid their wages. The assets have been privatized but the costs remain unpaid. The collapse of communism was world-shaking in its consequences. The victory may be short-lived, however, if ordinary citizens are denied the benefits associated with an "open society".

That is the issue. A society that is "open" only to the rich and powerful or a society "open" to everyone. One condition for the latter is that governments must remain sovereign. They must not allow the American or "Anglo-Saxon" model of unregulated capitalism to be foisted on an unsuspecting world through the MAI and other "trade" agreements. The second condition is for governments to reclaim sovereignty over part or all of the money-creation function. If they don't there will not be enough money available to finance a truly "open" society of opportunity for all.

Taxes are already too high and some immigrants are leaving Canada before they can be assessed on their overseas holdings. Any substantial increase in corporate taxes would see a renewed exodus. There is just nowhere to turn for the extra increment needed to care for the sick, the poor and the marginalized except government-created money. When this happens no one should weep for the banks who are already boasting that their big growth in income is coming from sources other than traditional banking.

A WORLD WHERE MARKETS REIGN

This is really a misnomer because it means a world poised to eliminate genuine market competition in many key areas; where banks merge and amalgamate to be in a better position to finance industrial mergers that eliminate jobs while, at the same time, losing interest in small businesses that create jobs.

It is a world where central bankers have more power than prime ministers and where money is more important than people. A world where private banks manufacture nearly all the money and thus have near total power over industry and governments — telling the latter what they may or may not do to help citizens displaced by technology or downsizing. It is a system where unemployment is high and total debt continues to increase because there is no way to repay it.

It is a world where the rich get richer and the poor get poorer because the trickle down theory of the '50s and '60s has been replaced by the trickle up theory. Every time central banks raise interest rates to slow the economy they raise the cost of borrowing for the poor and increase the rate of return on investments for the rich. Since 1974 there has been a massive trickling up of wealth from low income to high income groups.

Finally, it is a world where, for a lot of people, work has ceased to be fun. This is a common theme I hear everywhere I go. In September '96, Transport Minister David Anderson invited me to attend Transport Canada's 60th anniversary celebration. As it was inconvenient to go to Ottawa on November 1st, I participated in the Ontario Region party. Following the ceremony I chatted with officials about changes that had occurred over the years and their final words were: "It's not fun any more".

A group of Bank of Montreal employees in Vancouver made the same observation. They had been downsized to the point where there were several "nervous wrecks" from working extra hours in an attempt to cope. Nurses tell me the same thing. They are overworked and stressed out to the point that they know patient care is suffering. When 31-year old Maria Amaral started the 1997-98 school year at Holy Family Catholic School in Toronto's Parkdale district, with a class of 30 youngsters, she had the same complaint. The stress was getting to her and she realized it was impossible to give the children the individual attention they required.[5]

The absurdity of this situation is that these people are carrying the burden previously shared with colleagues who are now unemployed. It is a cruel system which creates a climate where nobody is happy — the unemployed because they have no jobs, and many who have jobs but are stretched to the breaking point.

A KINDER MORE DEMOCRATIC APPROACH

The distinguished American economist Robert Heilbröner points out that economics cannot be removed from a philosophical context. Certainly there is no moral or philosophical justification for the disconnect that is now occurring. The purpose of economic organization is not to provide a monopoly game for the few but to produce the goods and services essential for a healthy and challenging life for all. This is not to say that we should all have the same number of chips, but a declaration that the poor should not have to beg for the food necessary to keep body and soul intact.

A more democratic system would be one where anti-trust is alive and active in order that an element of genuine competition is maintained. There should be room in the world for big and small to coexist. Certainly there is a need for small banks to service the insatiable needs of small entrepreneurs. The amount of credit created for one or two large takeovers would be enough to finance thousands of small businesses that would create tens of thousands of jobs. In many parts of the underdeveloped world it is microbanking rather than big multinationals that would provide an answer to the prayers of the people.

Everyone longs for a job and opportunity. Any system which excludes large numbers of people is not as productive as it could be. So people who think in terms of overall efficiency should take the broad view.

JEREMY RIFKIN AND THE END OF WORK

As I have travelled across Canada and the U.S. preaching the gospel of monetary reform, one of the most frequent questions asked was whether I had read Rifkin's provocative book and, if so, how his ideas relate to what I have been saying. The answer is that I have read the book and there is a direct correlation between his concerns and the need for government-created money.

Although I consider Rifkin's views somewhat extreme, and believe that many new jobs can be created through demand management, there is no doubt that there are and will be marginalized workers with marginalized skills displaced by automation who will have nowhere to go. I also agree that the problem will intensify over the course of the next twenty years. Yet I have not heard of any political party or read any political platform that even pretends to address the situation.

Rifkin's solution is to pay the displaced workers to be volunteers. There would be three sectors — a private or market sector, a public or government sector and the volunteer sector. It is one solution. Another would be to have all levels of government compile lists of jobs that were useful but not essential in the sense that the public would not be seriously inconvenienced if the job was not filled. Occupations could include supervising outdoor rinks in winter, park maintenance, environmental clean-up, reforestation, answering telephones and providing information, holding the hands of the dying and so on. The list can be as long as your imagination and each job would provide, in some incremental way, a better quality of life for all.

Only one problem! Where is the money going to come from? The unregulated market which created the problem isn't going to accept responsibility. The extra taxes required to pay for these services would be considered oppressive. The only solution is to use some government-created money to help pay for the cost. It is a form of redistribution of income but a positive one because it's a win-win situation. The marginalized workers would gain self respect and income. The market would enjoy greater growth because these human beings, unlike robots, would want to buy food, clothing, shelter and a bit of recreation or entertainment with anything that was left over.

Any government which doesn't begin now to plan for the inevitable is, in a word, derelict.

WINTER AND SUMMER

The economic model that would best meet the world's needs would be one where governments provide the private sector with an institutional framework that supports prosperity. Partial reliance on government-created money would allow enhanced services and lower taxes simultaneously. In Canada most of the cuts to health care, education, environmental clean-up, science and research, the arts and the armed forces should be reinstated and the GST phased out over a period of three years. Computer simulations prove both are possible without any negative effect on the deficit.

Finally, a simple incomes policy tying union wages to the average increase in productivity, together with a requirement that big business pass the benefit of stable labor unit costs along to the consuming public, would allow all the developed world's economies to increase output by approximately 1 % more a year. This would mean hundreds of billions of dollars a year in extra output would be available — more than enough to address urgent domestic priorities and eliminate the most wretched poverty worldwide. In Canada alone the difference would be $8-billion per year which is not a sum to be sneezed at.

The practice of using interest rates to control inflation must end. An incomes policy is the most powerful tool but it can be supplemented by increasing the monthly minimum payable on credit cards, raising margin requirements on the purchase of stocks and bonds and increasing equity requirements on real estate transactions in the event the economy begins to overheat in one or more of these areas.

This second vision is one where everyone at least has a chance and where talent and hard work can compensate for the random chance of parentage. It is a system which would protect everyone from the ravages of misfortune beyond their control; where clean air, clean water and the good earth would be revered as much as bottom lines; where the extra 1% of output could be shared with less fortunate citizens of spaceship earth so that soon they, too, would have hope of a better life.

The international banks and multinational corporations, including a few Canadian ones, have made their decision in favor of unfettered laissez-faire capitalism. They are the instigators of the process conveniently dubbed "globalization", to mask its real intent. Their power and influence is already so great that they are using national governments as pawns.

Most of the rest of us have not bothered to choose because we have been brainwashed to believe that the process is inevitable and inexorable and there isn't a single thing we can do about it. That is not true! Until the MAI is signed there is still hope. Should the treaty be signed and ratified, heaven forbid, it will be too late.

CHAPTER 11

EMPOWERMENT

"They did not know it could not be done. So they did it."

Sir Tyrone Guthrie

I must admit that I have some difficulty with the word "empowerment" and found the dictionary explanation of little help. Yet I have a growing awareness of what people are thinking and feeling when they use it. It is the opposite to the sense of powerlessness that we all feel in the face of trends and events of which we disapprove but about which we feel that we can do nothing. We suspect we are being run over by an elite bureaucratic steamroller.

The issue was raised during the 1997 election campaign when I received several letters suggesting that with the advent of e-mail it should be possible to institute direct democracy and let the whole population vote on every issue before Parliament. This would be too time-consuming for most of us, however, so a compromise might be country-wide voting on the most critical issues. Certainly there are many who believe this should apply to constitutional reform where a referendum on the Charlottetown Accord showed public thinking to be out of sync with the views of officials and elected representatives.

Estrangement from the political process is the reason so many people are opting for referendum and recall in party platforms — especially people in Western Canada. In response, Prime Minister Chrétien said that there is a referendum in the form of an election once every four years and this is the average citizen's chance to pass judgement on the stewardship of his or her MP and of the government at large. Once the election is over, he implied, citizens disconnect and trust their government to serve them well.

There was a time, long ago, when I would have agreed with the Prime Minister. At the University of Toronto the indomitable professor MacGregor Dawson drilled into my mind the advantages of representative government. In between elections most citizens are too busy to study the merits of every issue so they must trust their MP to weigh the pros and cons and vote in their best interests.

The weakness in this excellent theory is the assumption that ordinary MPs count. Most of the time, they don't. They are expected to vote the party line which is determined by the Prime Minister, his office staff and a few senior cabinet ministers, all too often on the advice of faceless bureaucrats. That is the rule; a handful of senior officials set policy with little or no concern for ordinary people. Examples are legion.

If the high interest rate policy and induced recession of 1981-82 had been put to a vote in the Liberal caucus it would have been soundly defeated. The same with the 1990-92 recession and the Goods and Services Tax in the PC caucus. Had the Chrétien government advised caucus at the outset that its tight fiscal policy would eliminate half-a-million jobs, it probably would have been rejected although the propaganda barrage was so intense in this case that a lot of people did come to believe that deficit reduction by firing people was more important than deficit reduction by means of achieving full employment.

It is interesting to note that none of these policies were proposed by the parties at election time so they could be debated. Instead, it was jobs, jobs, jobs, at election time and the truth revealed later. The same is true in the case of the MAI. The Liberals, as I pointed out earlier, were at great pains not to debate it during the campaign and simply responded to any questions with brief, bland assurances. What is worse, most Liberal MPs were blithely unaware of what was going on and no one I talked to knew that two years of negotiations had already taken place. The government met concerns about the treaty with, "It's a year from signing so what's the worry?"

Any discussion of more power for the banks and the possibility of allowing them to merge was also on the verboten list and for very good reasons. The banks are not popular and any hint that the Liberals, like the Tories before them, had sold out would have created a powerfully negative pulse with the electorate. Yet reading between the lines, nothing stands in the way of bigger and fewer banks, with more power, except the passage of a little time during which we will be subject to another blast of propaganda about the imperatives of globalization.

MAN THE BARRICADES

Can these policies be reversed before they are set in concrete? Under normal circumstances I would say no, because a few speeches and letters to the editor won't make a dent on the combined power of the banks and the Ottawa autocracy. But these are not normal times because the future of Canada as a nation state is in jeopardy.

So, to take a leaf from Sir Tyrone Guthrie's reflection on the birth of the Shakespearean Festival at Stratford, "They did not know it could not be done, so they did it." We can stop the MAI if we want to badly enough. There is some magic number that would stop the government in its tracks and reverse the course of history. I know the number is not 5,000, or 10,000 or, perhaps, not even 100,000. But if the government received between 100,000 and 500,000 letters, faxes and e-mails from as many individuals saying, bluntly: "If you either sign the MAI or remove the 10% ownership limit on Canadian banks, without first having the policies approved by a binding referendum of the Canadian people, I promise that in the next election I will not vote for you or your party and will do everything within my power to defeat you," it might stop the train dead on its tracks. That many votes, adequately spread, might do for the Liberals what voters did to the Tories in 1993. It is the kind of sound even the deaf might hear.

All Canadian parties should oppose these policies so send a similar letter to your MP as well. The address is the same and no postage is required.

Rt. Hon. Jean Chrétien, P.C., M.P.
Prime Minister of Canada
House of Commons
Ottawa, ON K1A OA6

Dear Prime Minister:

I am quite distressed that the Multilateral Agreement on Investment was not seriously debated during the election campaign last Spring; also that the possibility of removing the 10% ownership rule for chartered banks was not discussed.

My reason for writing is to let you know that I am so concerned about these two issues that if either or both of them is approved in the absence of a binding referendum of the Canadian people I will not vote for you or your party in the next federal election and will do everything possible to defeat you.

I hope you will listen carefully and act accordingly.

Yours respectfully,

• • •

THE FINAL WORD

With the collapse of communism we dreamed of a world of hope and promise for all. Instead, we see a new "Evil Empire" extending its tentacles to embrace the horizons of the old one. It is an unfettered capitalism which is abandoning the kindly face it developed when it was competing in the battle for people's minds. It is a capitalism which proposes to run the world by its own rules for its own benefit — a system under which officers and shareholders of corporations win all the sweepstakes while the majority struggle to survive.

This trend, which is already well advanced, will be set in concrete when the MAI is signed in the Spring of 1988. If Canada succumbs, we will lose the power to run our country for the benefit of all Canadians. We will no longer have the power to say who can invest in our country, or under what conditions. Nor will there be any limit on how much of Canada foreigners can buy. Under the MAI they can buy it all!

This treaty is anathema to small and poor countries around the world. It would be a disaster for Canada. If we band together we can stop it. Then ordinary Canadians will have the final word.

NOTES

Chapter 2: An American Model

1.   From a table prepared by Professor Wallace Peterson, George Holmes Professor of Economics Emeritus, University of Nebraska — Lincoln.
2.   As reported in the *Globe and Mail*, June 19, 1997.
3.   As reported in the *New York Times*, February 28, 1997.
4.   Korten, David, "When Corporations Rule the World", October 12, 1996.
5.   As reported in the *Toronto Star*, July 10, 1997.
6.   As reported in the *Toronto Star*, June 24, 1997.
7.   Taken from an unpublished manuscript entitled "Double-Crossed by the Invisible Hand: Essays on the Behaviour of Money, the Public Interest and the Crash-Test Economy, by Keith Helmuth, Debec, New Brunswick, 1997.

Chapter 3: A Mediocre Canada

1.   Based on an interview with Mary Lippert.
2.   As reported in the *Toronto Star*, June 19, 1997.
3.   Press release by Ontario Nurses' Association, July 3, 1997.
4.   Brad Lavigne, "To the premiers: Help students out of the debt hole", *Globe and Mail*, August 1, 1997.
5.   As reported in the *Toronto Star*, June 27, 1997.
6.   As reported in the *Globe and Mail*, July 17, 1997.
7.   As reported in the *Toronto Star*, January 7, 1997.
8.   As reported in the *Toronto Star*, October 2, 1996.
9.   As reported in the *Globe and Mail*, April 8, 1996.

Chapter 4: About Money

1.   Hixson, William F., *Triumph of the Bankers: Money and Banking in the Eighteenth and Nineteenth Centuries*, Westport: Praeger Publishers, 1993.
2.   Chaffers, William, *Gilda Aurifabrorum: A History of English Goldsmiths and Plateworkers, and Their Marks Stamped on Plate*, London: Reeves & Turner, [1800].
3.   Nettles, Curtis P., *The Money Supply of the American Colonies before 1720*, New York: Augustus M. Kelley, 1964.
4.   Friedman, Milton, *A Program for Monetary Stability*, New York: Fordham University Press, 1959.

Chapter 5: A Disastrous Bank of Canada

1. In a speech to the Vancouver Board of Trade, October 7, 1997.
2. In his speech to the Montreal Board of Trade, January 19, 1995, the press interview following, and on other occasions.

Chapter 6: The Banks Play Monopoly

1. Sir Josiah Stamp, Later Baron Stamp, was a director of the Bank of England from 1928-1941.
2. Bank of Canada Review, Summer 1997, p. 47.
3. As reported in the *Vancouver Sun*, September 9, 1997.
4. As reported in the *Financial Post*, August 12, 1996.
5. As reported in the *Toronto Star*, October 3, 1996.
6. *Globe and Mail* lead editorial, June 20, 1997.
7. Bank of Montreal, "Policy Alternatives for Canadian Financial Services", July, 1997.

Chapter 7: A F Grade for the Media

1. Sonnen, Carl, "A Strategy for Sustained, Full-Employment Growth Without Inflation", Informetrica Limited, March 31, 1993.
2. Hellyer diary, December 6, 1994.
3. Downing, John, "Hellyer's economic 'heresy' is just ... Dollars and sense," *Toronto Sun*, March 12, 1995.
4. Minvielle, Paul, "Listen hard to Hellyer's message," *Times Colonist*, Victoria, March 20, 1997.
5. Ibid.

Chapter 8: Globalization: The Evil Empire

1. Clayton Yeutter was the Chief U.S. Trade Representative at the time the Free Trade Agreement was signed in October 1987.
2. As reported in the *Toronto Star*, May 23, 1996.
3. *Ibid*.
4. List compiled by Professor John McMurtry, Department of Philosophy, University of Guelph, for the Interdisciplinary Conference on the Evolution of World Order; Building a Foundation of Peace in the Third Millenium.
5. Clark, Tony, The Corporate Rule Treaty. Ottawa, The Canadian Centre for Policy Alternatives, 1994, p. 4.
6. As reported in the *Toronto Star*, June 10, 1997.
7. As reported in the *Toronto Star*, September 22, 1997.

Chapter 10: The 21st Century

1.   David Korten taught at the Harvard Business School, worked for the Ford Foundation and the U.S. Agency for International Development. He is now president of the People-Centered Development Forum. He is the author of *When Corporations Rule the World.*

2.   As reported in the *New York Times*, February 14, 1996.

3.   From "Ideological pendulum swings back to centre", a column by Monique Jérôme Forget, president of the Institute for Research on Public Policy, *The Financial Post*, May 31, 1997.

4.   From the *Atlantic Monthly*, January, 1997.

5.   As reported in the *Toronto Star*, October 6, 1997.

RECOMMENDED READING

Biddell, Jack L., *A Self-Reliant Future for Canada.*   Thornhill: LNC Publications, 1993.

Figgie, Harry E. Jr., *Bankruptcy 1995: The Coming Collapse of America and How to Stop It.* Boston, Toronto: Little Brown, 1992.

Hellyer, Paul, *Surviving the Global Financial Crisis: The Economics of Hope for Generation X.* Toronto: Chimo Media, 1996.

Hellyer, Paul, *Funny Money: A Common Sense Alternative to Mainline Economics.* Toronto: Chimo Media, 1994.

Hixson, William F., *It's your Money.* Toronto: COMER Publications, 1997.

Hixson, William F., *Triumph of the Bankers: Money and Banking in the Eighteenth and Nineteenth Centuries.* Westport: Praeger Publishers, 1993.

Hixson, William, F., *A Matter of Interest: Reexamining Money, Debt, and Real Economic Growth.* New York: Praeger Publishers, 1991.

Krehm, William, *A Power Unto Itself: The Bank of Canada.* Toronto: Stoddard Publishing Co. Limited, 1993.

Pope, William Henry, *All You Must Know About Economics.* Toronto: COMER Publications, 1996.

Phillips, Ronnie J., *The Chicago Plan & New Deal Banking Reform.* New York: M.E. Sharpe, Inc., 1995.

Stewart, Walter, *Bank Heist: How Our Financial Giants Are Costing You Money.* Toronto: HarperCollins Publishers Ltd., 1997.

Thauberger, J.A., *Inflation: Bankrupcties, Unemployment Can Be Beaten,* The New World Publishing Company, 1983.

INDEX